Sing to the Lord
Music in Divine Worship

Sing to the Lord
Music in Divine Worship

PASTORAL LITURGY SERIES • **FOUR**

UNITED STATES CONFERENCE OF CATHOLIC BISHOPS
Washington, D.C.

Sing to the Lord: Music in Divine Worship was developed by the Music Subcommittee of the Committee on Divine Worship of the United States Conference of Catholic Bishops (USCCB). It was approved for publication by the full body of bishops at its November 2007 General Meeting and has been authorized for publication by the undersigned.

Msgr. David J. Malloy, STD
General Secretary, USCCB

Cover photo: Michael Hoyt, *Catholic Standard* newspaper, Washington, D.C.

ISBN 978-1-60137-022-8

First printing, June 2008

Contents

Abbreviations

AG	Second Vatican Council, *Ad Gentes Divinitus* (*Decree on the Church's Missionary Activity*) (1965)
BCL	Bishops' Committee on the Liturgy (now the Committee on Divine Worship)
BLS	USCCB, *Built of Living Stones: Art, Architecture, and Worship* (2000)
CCC	*Catechism of the Catholic Church*, 2nd edition
CVL	USCCB, *Co-Workers in the Vineyard of the Lord: A Resource for Guiding the Development of Lay Ecclesial Ministry* (2005)
DV	Second Vatican Council, *Dei Verbum* (*Dogmatic Constitution on Divine Revelation*) (1965)
GILH	*General Instruction of the Liturgy of the Hours*
GIRM	*General Instruction of the Roman Missal*
GS	Second Vatican Council, *Gaudium et Spes* (*Pastoral Constitution on the Church in the Modern World*) (1965)
HCWEOM	*Holy Communion and Worship of the Eucharist Outside Mass*
LFM	*Lectionary for Mass*
LTA	John Paul II, *Letter to Artists* (1999)
MS	Sacred Congregation for Rites, *Musicam Sacram* (*Instruction on Music in the Liturgy*) (1967)

MSD   Pius XII, *Musicae Sacrae Disciplina* (*On Sacred Music*) (1955)

OCF   *Order of Christian Funerals*

ORD   *Rites of Ordination of a Bishop, of Priests, and of Deacons,* 2nd typical edition

PCS   *Pastoral Care of the Sick*

PL   *Patrologiae cursus completes: Series Latina*

RBC   *Rite of Baptism of Children*

RC   *Rite of Confirmation*

RCIA   *Rite of Christian Initiation of Adults*

RM   *Rite of Marriage*

SacCar   Benedict XVI, *Sacramentum Caritatis* (*Sacrament of Charity*) (2007)

SC   Second Vatican Council, *Sacrosanctum Concilium* (*Constitution on the Sacred Liturgy*) (1963)

USCCB   United States Conference of Catholic Bishops

Sing to the Lord: Music in Divine Worship, a revision of *Music in Catholic Worship*, was developed by the Music Subcommittee of the Committee on Divine Worship of the United States Conference of Catholic Bishops (USCCB). On November 14, 2007, the Latin Church members of the USCCB approved these guidelines. These guidelines are designed to provide direction to those preparing for the celebration of the Sacred Liturgy according to the current liturgical books (in the ordinary form of celebration).

Foreword

Greetings from the bishops of the United States to priests, deacons, liturgists, music directors, composers, cantors, choirs, congregations, and faith communities throughout the United States. "Grace to you and peace from God our Father and the Lord Jesus Christ."[1] It is our duty and our joy as shepherds of the Church to guide and oversee liturgical song in each particular Church. Liturgy is the source of the Church's prayer and action, and the summit by which our lives and all our ministries ascend to the Father. We pray that this document will draw all who worship the Lord into the fullness of liturgical, musical prayer.

---

1   Eph 1:1.

4. Jesus and his apostles sang a hymn before their journey to the Mount of Olives.[9] St. Paul instructed the Ephesians to "[address] one another in psalms and hymns and spiritual songs, singing and playing to the Lord in your hearts."[10] He sang with Silas in captivity.[11] The letter of St. James asks, "Is anyone among you suffering? He should pray. Is anyone in good spirits? He should sing praise."[12]

5. Obedient to Christ and to the Church, we gather in liturgical assembly, week after week. As our predecessors did, we find ourselves "singing psalms, hymns and spiritual songs with gratitude in [our] hearts to God."[13] This common, sung expression of faith within liturgical celebrations strengthens our faith when it grows weak and draws us into the divinely inspired voice of the Church at prayer. Faith grows when it is well expressed in celebration. Good celebrations can foster and nourish faith. Poor celebrations may weaken it. Good music "make[s] the liturgical prayers of the Christian community more alive and fervent so that everyone can praise and beseech the Triune God more powerfully, more intently and more effectively."[14]

6. "In human life, signs and symbols occupy an important place. As a being at once body and spirit, man expresses and perceives spiritual realities through physical signs and symbols. . . . Inasmuch as they are creatures, these perceptible realities can become means of expressing the action of God who sanctifies men, and the action of men who offer worship to God."[15] This sacramental principle is the consistent belief of the

---

9   See Mt 26:30; Mk 14:26.

10   Eph 5:18-19.

11   "About midnight . . . Paul and Silas were praying and singing hymns to God, as the other prisoners listened" (Acts 16:25).

12   Jas 5:13.

13   Col 3:16; see *General Instruction of the Roman Missal* (GIRM), no. 39 (Washington, DC: United States Conference of Catholic Bishops [USCCB], 2003). See Eph 5:19.

14   MSD, no. 31; see no. 33.

15   *Catechism of the Catholic Church* (CCC), 2nd ed., nos. 1146, 1148 (Washington, DC: Libreria Editrice Vaticana–USCCB, 2000).

Church throughout history. In Liturgy, we use words, gestures, signs, and symbols to proclaim Christ's presence and to reply with our worship and praise.

7. The primordial song of the Liturgy is the canticle of victory over sin and death. It is the song of the saints, standing beside "the sea of glass": "They were holding God's harps, and they sang the song of Moses, the servant of God, and the song of the Lamb."[16] "Liturgical singing is established in the midst of this great historical tension. For Israel, the event of salvation in the Red Sea will always be the main reason for praising God, the basic theme of the songs it sings before God. For Christians, the Resurrection of Christ is the true Exodus. . . . The definitively new song has been intoned. . . ."[17]

8. The Paschal hymn, of course, does not cease when a liturgical celebration ends. Christ, whose praises we have sung, remains with us and leads us through church doors to the whole world, with its joys and hopes, griefs and anxieties.[18] The words Jesus chose from the book of Isaiah at the beginning of his ministry become the song of the Body of Christ. "The Spirit of the Lord is upon me, / because he has anointed me / to bring glad tidings to the poor. / He has sent me to proclaim liberty to / captives and recovery of sight to the blind, / to let the oppressed go free, / and to proclaim a year acceptable to the Lord."[19]

9. Charity, justice, and evangelization are thus the normal consequences of liturgical celebration. Particularly inspired by sung participation, the body of the Word Incarnate goes forth to spread the Gospel with full force and compassion. In this way, the Church leads men and women "to the faith, freedom and peace of Christ by the example of its life and

---

16   Rev 15:3.

17   Cardinal Joseph Ratzinger, *The Spirit of the Liturgy* (Ignatius Press, 2000), 137-138.

18   See Second Vatican Council, *Gaudium et Spes* (*Pastoral Constitution on the Church in the Modern World*) (GS), no. 1, in *Vatican Council II: The Conciliar and Post Conciliar Documents*, new revised edition, ed. Austin Flannery, OP (Northport, NY: Costello Publishing, 1996). All subsequent Second Vatican Council passages come from the Flannery edition.

19   Lk 4:18; see Is 61:1-2, 58:6.

teaching, by the sacraments and other means of grace. Its aim is to open up for all men a free and sure path to full participation in the mystery of Christ."[20]

Participation

10. Holy Mother Church clearly affirms the role within worship of the entire liturgical assembly (bishop, priest, deacon, acolytes, ministers of the Word, music leaders, choir, extraordinary ministers of Holy Communion, and the congregation). Through grace, the liturgical assembly partakes in the life of the Blessed Trinity, which is itself a communion of love. In a perfect way, the Persons of the Trinity remain themselves even as they share all that they are. For our part, "we, though many, are one body in Christ and individually parts of one another."[21] The Church urges all members of the liturgical assembly to receive this divine gift and to participate fully "depending on their orders [and] their role in the liturgical services."[22]

11. Within the gathered assembly, the role of the congregation is especially important. "The full and active participation by all the people is the aim to be considered before all else, for it is the primary and indispensable source from which the faithful are to derive the true Christian spirit."[23]

12. Participation in the Sacred Liturgy must be "internal, in the sense that by it the faithful join their mind to what they pronounce or hear, and cooperate with heavenly grace."[24] Even when listening to the various prayers and readings of the Liturgy or to the singing of the choir, the assembly continues to participate actively as they "unite themselves

---

20   Second Vatican Council, *Ad Gentes Divinitus* (*Decree on the Church's Missionary Activity*) (AG), no. 5.

21   Rom 12:5-6.

22   Second Vatican Council, *Sacrosanctum Concilium* (*Constitution on the Sacred Liturgy*) (SC), no. 26.

23   SC, no. 14.

24   Sacred Congregation for Rites, *Musicam Sacram* (*Instruction on Music in the Liturgy*) (MS), no. 15, in Flannery, *Vatican Council II*; see SC, no. 11.

interiorly to what the ministers or choir sing, so that by listening to them they may raise their minds to God."[25] "In a culture which neither favors nor fosters meditative quiet, the art of interior listening is learned only with difficulty. Here we see how the liturgy, though it must always be properly inculturated, must also be counter-cultural."[26]

13. Participation must also be external, so that internal participation can be expressed and reinforced by actions, gestures, and bodily attitudes, and by the acclamations, responses, and singing.[27] The quality of our participation in such sung praise comes less from our vocal ability than from the desire of our hearts to sing together of our love for God. Participation in the Sacred Liturgy both expresses and strengthens the faith that is in us.

14. Our participation in the Liturgy is challenging. Sometimes, our voices do not correspond to the convictions of our hearts. At other times, we are distracted or preoccupied by the cares of the world. Christ always invites us, however, to enter into song, to rise above our own preoccupations, and to give our entire selves to the hymn of his Paschal Sacrifice for the honor and glory of the Most Blessed Trinity.

---

25   MS, no. 15.

26   Pope John Paul II, Address to Bishops of the Northwest Provinces of the USCCB, in *Ad Limina Addresses: The Addresses of His Holiness Pope John Paul II to the Bishops of the United States, February 1998–October 1998* (Washington, DC: USCCB, 1998), no. 3.

27   See SC, no. 30.

II. The Church at Prayer

15. The Church is always at prayer in her ministers and her people, and that prayer takes various forms in her life. Authentic sacred music supports the Church's prayer by enriching its elements. What follows below are the principal persons and elements that should guide both the development and the use of sacred music in the Liturgy.

A. The Bishop

16. In his capacity as "the chief steward of the mysteries of God in the particular Church entrusted to his care,"[28] the diocesan bishop is particularly concerned with the promotion of the dignity of liturgical celebrations, "the beauty of the sacred place, of music, and of art."[29] He carries out this duty through the example of his own celebration of the Sacred Liturgy, encouraging sung participation by his own example; by his attention to the practice of liturgical music in the parishes and communities of his diocese, especially in his own cathedral church; by his promotion of the continuing musical education and formation of clergy and musicians; and by his careful attention to the musical training of future priests and deacons.

17. The bishop is assisted in this role by his staff in the diocesan Office of Worship and/or the diocesan music or liturgical commission, which provides "valuable assistance in promoting sacred music together with pastoral liturgical action in the diocese."[30]

---

28   GIRM, no. 22.
29   GIRM, no. 22.
30   MS, no. 68.

B. The Priest

18. No other single factor affects the Liturgy as much as the attitude, style, and bearing of the priest celebrant, who "prays in the name of the Church and of the assembled community."[31] "When he celebrates the Eucharist, . . . [the priest] must serve God and the people with dignity and humility, and by his bearing and by the way he says the divine words he must convey to the faithful the living presence of Christ."[32]

19. The importance of the priest's participation in the Liturgy, especially by singing, cannot be overemphasized. The priest sings the presidential prayers and dialogues of the Liturgy according to his capabilities,[33] and he encourages sung participation in the Liturgy by his own example, joining in the congregational song. "If, however . . . the priest or minister does not possess a voice suitable for the proper execution of the singing, he can render without singing one or more of the more difficult parts which concern him, reciting them in a loud and distinct voice. However, this must not be done merely for the convenience of the priest or minister."[34]

20. Seminaries and other programs of priestly formation should train priests to sing with confidence and to chant those parts of the Mass assigned to them. Those priests who are capable should be trained in the practice of chanting the Gospel on more solemn occasions when a deacon may not be present. At the very least, all priests should be comfortable singing those parts of the Eucharistic Prayer that are assigned to them for which musical notation is provided in the *Roman Missal*.[35]

---

31   GIRM, no. 33.
32   GIRM, no. 93.
33   The documents of the post-conciliar liturgical renewal repeatedly commend the ideal of a sung Liturgy with sung dialogues between priest and people, such as *The Lord be with you*, the acclamation at the end of the Gospel, and the introductory dialogue to the Eucharistic Prayer. See MS, nos. 29-31; *Lectionary for Mass (Second Typical Edition): Introduction* (LFM) (Washington, DC: USCCB, 1998), no. 17; GIRM, no. 40.
34   MS, no. 8.
35   See GIRM, no. 147.

21. The priest joins with the congregation in singing the acclamations, chants, hymns, and songs of the Liturgy. However, the priest does not join in the singing of the Memorial Acclamation or the Great Amen. To the greatest extent possible, he should use a congregational worship aid during the processions and other rituals of the Liturgy and should be attentive to the cantor and psalmist as they lead the gathered assembly in song. In order to promote the corporate voice of the assembly when it sings, the priest's own voice should not be heard above the congregation, nor should he sing the congregational response of the dialogues. While the assembly sings, the priest should step back from a microphone, or, if he is using a wireless microphone, he should turn it off.

C. The Deacon

22. After the priest, the deacon is first among the liturgical ministers, and he should provide an example by actively participating in the song of the gathered assembly.[36]

23. In accord with their abilities, deacons should be prepared to sing those parts of the Liturgy that belong to them. Deacons should receive training in singing the dialogues between deacon and people, such as those at the Gospel and at the dismissal. They should also learn to sing various invitations in the rites, the *Exsultet*, the third form of the Act of Penitence, and the Prayer of the Faithful. If they are capable, deacons should be trained in the practice of chanting the Gospel on more solemn occasions. Programs of diaconal formation should include major and compulsory courses in the chant and song of the Liturgy.

---

36   See GIRM, no. 94.

D. The Gathered Liturgical Assembly

24. "In the celebration of Mass the faithful form a holy people, a people whom God has made his own, a royal priesthood, so that they may give thanks to God and offer the spotless Victim not only through the hands of the priest but also together with him, and so that they may learn to offer themselves."[37] This is the basis for the "full, conscious and active participation" of the faithful demanded by the very nature of the Liturgy.[38]

25. Because the gathered liturgical assembly forms one body, each of its members must shun "any appearance of individualism or division, keeping before their eyes that they have only one Father in heaven and accordingly are all brothers and sisters to each other."[39]

26. Singing is one of the primary ways that the assembly of the faithful participates actively in the Liturgy. The people are encouraged "to take part by means of acclamations, responses, psalms, antiphons [and] hymns. . . ."[40] The musical formation of the assembly must be a continuing concern in order to foster full, conscious, and active participation.

27. So that the holy people may sing with one voice, the music must be within its members' capability. Some congregations are able to learn more quickly and will desire more variety. Others will be more comfortable with a stable number of songs so that they can be at ease when they sing. Familiarity with a stable repertoire of liturgical songs rich in theological content can deepen the faith of the community through repetition and memorization. A pastoral judgment must be made in all cases.

---

37   GIRM, no. 95.
38   See SC, no. 14.
39   GIRM, no. 95.
40   SC, no. 30.

E. Ministers of Liturgical Music

The Choir

28. The Second Vatican Council stated emphatically that choirs must be diligently promoted while ensuring that "the whole body of the faithful may be able to contribute that active participation which is rightly theirs. . . ."[41] The choir must not minimize the musical participation of the faithful. The congregation commonly sings unison melodies, which are more suitable for generally unrehearsed community singing. This is the primary song of the Liturgy. Choirs and ensembles, on the other hand, comprise persons drawn from the community who possess the requisite musical skills and a commitment to the established schedule of rehearsals and liturgies. Thus, they are able to enrich the celebration by adding musical elements beyond the capabilities of the congregation alone.

29. Choirs (and ensembles—another form of choir that commonly includes a combination of singers and instrumentalists) exercise their ministry in various ways. An important ministerial role of the choir or ensemble is to sing various parts of the Mass in dialogue or alternation with the congregation. Some parts of the Mass that have the character of a litany, such as the *Kyrie* and the *Agnus Dei,* are clearly intended to be sung in this manner. Other Mass parts may also be sung in dialogue or alternation, especially the *Gloria*, the Creed, and the three processional songs: the Entrance, the Preparation of the Gifts, and Communion. This approach often takes the form of a congregational refrain with verses sung by the choir. Choirs may also enrich congregational singing by adding harmonies and descants.

30. At times, the choir performs its ministry by singing alone. The choir may draw on the treasury of sacred music, singing compositions by composers of various periods and in various musical styles, as well as music that expresses the faith of the various cultures that enrich the Church. Appropriate times when the choir might commonly sing alone include a prelude before Mass, the Entrance chant, the Preparation of

---

41   SC, no. 114.

the Gifts, during the Communion procession or after the reception of Communion, and the recessional. Other appropriate examples are given in the section of this document entitled "Music and the Structure of the Mass" (nos. 137-199). The music of the choir must always be appropriate to the Liturgy, either by being a proper liturgical text or by expressing themes appropriate to the Liturgy.

31. When the choir is not exercising its particular role, it joins the congregation in song. The choir's role in this case is not to lead congregational singing, but to sing with the congregation, which sings on its own or under the leadership of the organ or other instruments.

32. Choir members, like all liturgical ministers, should exercise their ministry with evident faith and should participate in the entire liturgical celebration, recognizing that they are servants of the Liturgy and members of the gathered assembly.

33. Choir and ensemble members may dress in albs or choir robes, but always in clean, presentable, and modest clothing. Cassock and surplice, being clerical attire, are not recommended as choir vesture.

The Psalmist

34. The psalmist, or "cantor of the psalm," proclaims the Psalm after the first reading and leads the gathered assembly in singing the refrain.[42] The psalmist may also, when necessary, intone the Gospel Acclamation and verse.[43] Although this ministry is distinct from the role of the cantor, the two ministries are often entrusted to the same person.

35. Persons designated for the ministry of psalmist should possess "the ability for singing and a facility in correct pronunciation and diction."[44] As one who proclaims the Word, the psalmist should be able to proclaim the text of the Psalm with clarity, conviction, and sensitivity to the text, the musical setting, and those who are listening.

---

42   LFM, no. 56.
43   See LFM, no. 56.
44   GIRM, no. 102. See LFM, no. 56.

36. The psalmist sings the verses of the Responsorial Psalm from the ambo or another suitable place.[45] The psalmist may dress in an alb or choir robe, but always wears clean, presentable, and modest clothing. Cassock and surplice, being clerical attire, are not recommended as vesture for the psalmist.

The Cantor

37. The cantor is both a singer and a leader of congregational song. Especially when no choir is present, the cantor may sing in alternation or dialogue with the assembly. For example, the cantor may sing the invocations of the *Kyrie*, intone the *Gloria*, lead the short acclamations at the end of the Scripture readings, intone and sing the verse of the Gospel Acclamation, sing the invocations of the Prayer of the Faithful, and lead the singing of the *Agnus Dei*. The cantor may also sing the verses of the psalm or song that accompany the Entrance, Preparation of the Gifts, and Communion. Finally, the cantor may serve as psalmist, leading and proclaiming the verses of the Responsorial Psalm.

38. As a leader of congregational song, the cantor should take part in singing with the entire gathered assembly. In order to promote the singing of the liturgical assembly, the cantor's voice should not be heard above the congregation. As a transitional practice, the voice of the cantor might need to be amplified to stimulate and lead congregational singing when this is still weak. However, as the congregation finds its voice and sings with increasing confidence, the cantor's voice should correspondingly recede. At times, it may be appropriate to use a modest gesture that invites participation and clearly indicates when the congregation is to begin, but gestures should be used sparingly and only when genuinely needed.

39. Cantors should lead the assembly from a place where they can be seen by all without drawing attention from the liturgical action. When, however, a congregation is singing very familiar responses, acclamations,

---

45   See GIRM, no. 61.

or songs that do not include verses for the cantor alone, the cantor need not be visible.

40. The cantor exercises his or her ministry from a conveniently located stand, but not from the ambo.[46] The cantor may dress in an alb or choir robe, but always in clean, presentable, and modest clothing. Cassock and surplice, being clerical attire, are not recommended as vesture for the cantor.

The Organist and the Other Instrumentalists

41. The primary role of the organist, other instrumentalists, or instrumental ensemble is to lead and sustain the singing of the assembly and of the choir, cantor, and psalmist, without dominating or overpowering them.

42. The many voices of the organ and of instrumental ensembles, with their great range of expression, add varied and colorful dimensions to the song of the assembly, especially with the addition of harmonization.

43. Those with the requisite talent and training should be encouraged to continue the musical tradition of improvisation. The liturgical action may call for improvisation, for example, when a congregational hymn or choral piece concludes before the ritual action is completed. The art of improvisation requires its own special talent and training. More than mere background sound is called for. When worthy improvisation is not possible, it is recommended that musicians play quality published literature, which is available at all levels of difficulty.

44. There are also times when the organ or other instruments may be played alone, such as a prelude before the Mass, an instrumental piece during the Preparation of the Gifts, a recessional if there is no closing song, or a postlude following a closing song.

---

46   See LFM, no. 33.

The Director of Music Ministries

45. A professional director of music ministries, or music director, provides a major service by working with the bishop or pastor to oversee the planning, coordination, and ministries of the parish or diocesan liturgical music program. The director of music ministries fosters the active participation of the liturgical assembly in singing; coordinates the preparation of music to be sung at various liturgical celebrations; and promotes the ministries of choirs, psalmists, cantors, organists, and all who play instruments that serve the Liturgy. In the present day, many potential directors of music are not of our faith tradition. It is significant as we go forward that directors of music are properly trained to express our faith traditions effectively and with pastoral sensitivity.

46. Since every ministry is rooted in the Sacraments of Initiation, which form the People of God into "a community of disciples formed by and for the mission of Christ,"[47] the director of music ministries has a role that "finds its place within the communion of the Church and serves the mission of Christ in the Spirit."[48]

47. Directors of music ministries and other lay ecclesial ministers exercise their role in relation both to the ordained and to the community of the faithful. Directors are collaborators with bishops, priests, and deacons, who exercise a pastoral ministry based on the Sacrament of Holy Orders, which configures them to Christ the Head and consecrates them for a role that is unique and necessary for the communion of the Church.[49] At the same time, lay ecclesial ministers are members of the lay faithful, "sharing in the common priesthood of all the baptized" and "called to discipleship."[50]

---

47   USCCB, *Co-Workers in the Vineyard of the Lord: A Resource for Guiding the Development of Lay Ecclesial Ministry* (CVL) (Washington, DC: USCCB, 2005), 21.

48   CVL, 17.

49   See CVL, 21ff.; CCC, no. 1581.

50   CVL, 25.

F. Leadership and Formation

48. The whole assembly is actively involved in the music of the Liturgy. Some members of the community, however, are recognized for the special gifts they exhibit in leading the musical praise and thanksgiving of Christian assemblies. These are the liturgical musicians, as described in section E, above, and their ministry is especially cherished by the Church.

49. Liturgical musicians are first of all disciples, and only then are they ministers. Joined to Christ through the Sacraments of Initiation, musicians belong to the assembly of the baptized faithful; they are worshipers above all else. Like other baptized members of the assembly, pastoral musicians need to hear the Gospel, experience conversion, profess faith in Christ, and so proclaim the praise of God. Thus, musicians who serve the Church at prayer are not merely employees or volunteers. They are ministers who share the faith, serve the community, and express the love of God and neighbor through music.

50. All pastoral musicians—professional or volunteer, full-time or part-time, director or choir member, cantor or instrumentalist—exercise a genuine liturgical ministry.[51] The community of the faithful has a right to expect that this service will be provided competently. Pastoral musicians should receive appropriate formation that is based on their baptismal call to discipleship; that grounds them in a love for and knowledge of Scripture, Catholic teaching, Liturgy, and music; and that equips them with the musical, liturgical, and pastoral skills to serve the Church at prayer.

51. Preparation for music ministry should include appropriate human formation, spiritual formation, intellectual formation, and pastoral formation.[52] Bishops and pastors should encourage liturgical musicians to take part in ministerial formation opportunities offered by universities, colleges, seminaries, ministry formation programs, dioceses, and national

---

51   See SC, no. 29.
52   CVL, 33-53.

ministry associations. Parishes and dioceses should provide the financial support needed to ensure competent liturgical musical leadership.

52. The service of pastoral musicians should be recognized as a valued and integral part of the overall pastoral ministry of the parish or diocese; provision should be made for just compensation. Professional directors of music ministries and part-time pastoral music ministers should each receive appropriate wages and benefits that affirm the dignity of their work.[53]

53. Liturgical music ministers should be provided with the proper resources to carry out their administrative functions in a professional manner.

G. Music in Catholic Schools

54. Catholic educational institutions have a special obligation toward music and the Sacred Liturgy. Catholic schools are called to foster the joy of singing and making music, to cultivate the repertoire of sacred music inherited from the past, to engage the creative efforts of contemporary composers and the diverse repertoires of various cultures, and to celebrate the Sacred Liturgy worthily.

55. Catholic grade schools and high schools, which sometimes have students from several parishes and a variety of faith traditions, should at a minimum help all of their students to become singers. Singing should be a regular part of the school day, e.g., in homeroom, in music classes, and at school assemblies. School Liturgies, while appropriate to the age level of the participants, should follow the prescriptions of nos. 110-114 in this document, and the other relevant guidelines on sacred music. Choirs should be promoted, and their ministry should be employed regularly at school Liturgies in accord with nos. 28-33. A variety of musical styles is recommended at school Liturgies, while care should be taken to include

---

53   CVL, 63.

selections from the repertoire typically sung by the wider Church at Sunday Liturgies. In this way, students will be introduced to music they will sing throughout their life, and they will be better prepared for their eventual role as adult members of the worshiping assembly.

56. Catholic colleges and universities show that they come "from the heart of the Church"[54] especially in their worthy celebration of the Church's Liturgy, which should be a priority at every Catholic school. Catholic institutions of higher education should cultivate a high level of musical skill and a broad range of repertoire at campus Liturgies, and they should strive to make use of the talents of the entire academic community, especially music students and faculty, while taking care to include selections from the repertoire typically sung by the wider Church at Sunday Liturgies.

H. Diverse Cultures and Languages

57. Even as the liturgical music of the Western European tradition is to be remembered, cherished, and used, the rich cultural and ethnic heritage of the many peoples of our country must also be recognized, fostered, and celebrated. Cultural pluralism has been the common heritage of all Americans, and "the Catholic community is rapidly re-encountering itself as an immigrant Church."[55] "The cultural gifts of the new immigrants" are "taking their place alongside those of older generations of immigrants,"[56] and this calls for interaction and collaboration between peoples who speak various languages and celebrate their faith in the songs and musical styles of their cultural, ethnic, and racial roots. In order to do so effectively, music publishers need to be encouraged to offer multilingual options for use which would be more expressive of our unity amidst such great diversity.

---

54   See John Paul II, Apostolic Constitution *Ex Corde Ecclesiae* (*On Catholic Colleges and Universities*) (1990).

55   USCCB, *Welcoming the Stranger: Unity in Diversity* (Washington, DC: USCCB, 2000), 7.

56   *Welcoming the Stranger*, 16.

58. Liturgical music must always be chosen and sung "with due consideration for the culture of the people and abilities of each liturgical assembly."[57] Immigrants should be welcomed and should be provided with the resources they need to worship in their own language. "Religious singing by the faithful is to be intelligently fostered so that in devotions and sacred exercises as well as in liturgical services, the voices of the faithful may be heard, in conformity with the norms and requirements of the rubrics."[58] However, as the second generation of an immigrant group comes to maturity in the worshiping assembly, bilingual (native language and English) resources and songs are needed to promote participation of the multicultural and multigenerational assembly.

59. As dioceses, parishes, and neighborhoods become increasingly diverse, the different cultural groups strive for some expression of unity. In a spirit of hospitality, local worshiping communities are encouraged to develop bicultural or multicultural celebrations from time to time that reflect the changing face of the Church in America. When prepared with an attitude of mutual reciprocity, local communities might eventually expand from those celebrations that merely highlight their multicultural differences to celebrations that better reflect the intercultural relationships of the assembly and the unity that is shared in Christ. Likewise, the valuable musical gifts of the diverse cultural and ethnic communities should enrich the whole Church in the United States by contributing to the repertory of liturgical song and to the growing richness of Christian faith.

60. Liturgical music today must reflect the multicultural diversity and intercultural relationships of the members of the gathered liturgical assembly. The varied use of musical forms such as ostinato refrains, call and response, song translations, and bilingual or multilingual repertoire can assist in weaving the diverse languages and ethnicities of the liturgical assembly into a tapestry of sung praise. Liturgical leaders and musicians should encourage not only the use of traditional music of other

---

57   GIRM, no. 40.
58   SC, no. 118.

languages and peoples, but also the incorporation of newly composed liturgical music appropriate to various cultural expressions in harmony with the theological meaning of the rites. Care should be taken, however, to choose appropriate hymns in other languages so as to avoid an expression that could be misconstrued as tokenism.

I. Latin in the Liturgy

61. The use of the vernacular is the norm in most liturgical celebrations in the dioceses of the United States "for the sake of a better comprehension of the mystery being celebrated."[59] However, care should be taken to foster the role of Latin in the Liturgy, particularly in liturgical song. Pastors should ensure "that the faithful may also be able to say or to sing together in Latin those parts of the Ordinary of the Mass which pertain to them."[60] They should be able to sing these parts of the Mass proper to them, at least according to the simpler melodies.

62. At international and multicultural gatherings of different language groups, it is most appropriate to celebrate the Liturgy in Latin, "with the exception of the readings, the homily and the prayer of the faithful."[61] In addition, "selections of Gregorian chant should be sung" at such gatherings, whenever possible.[62]

63. To facilitate the singing of texts in Latin, the singers should be trained in its correct pronunciation and understand its meaning. To the greatest extent possible and applicable, singers and choir directors are encouraged to deepen their familiarity with the Latin language.

---

59   GIRM, no. 12.
60   SC, no. 54; see MS, no. 47; Sacred Congregation for Rites, *Inter Oecumenici* (*Instruction on the Proper Implementation of the Constitution on the Sacred Liturgy*), no. 59, in Flannery, *Vatican Council II.*
61   Pope Benedict XVI, Post-Synodal Apostolic Exhortation *Sacramentum Caritatis* (*The Sacrament of Charity*) (SacCar) (Washington, DC: USCCB, 2007), no. 62.
62   SacCar, no. 62.

64. Whenever the Latin language poses an obstacle to singers, even after sufficient training has been provided—for example, in pronunciation, understanding of the text, or confident rendition of a piece—it would be more prudent to employ a vernacular language in the Liturgy.

65. Seminarians should "receive the preparation needed to understand and to celebrate Mass in Latin, and also to use Latin texts and execute Gregorian chant."[63]

66. In promoting the use of Latin in the Liturgy, pastors should always "employ that form of participation which best matches the capabilities of each congregation."[64]

---

63   SacCar, no. 62.
64   MS, no. 47.

III. The Music of Catholic Worship

A. Different Kinds of Music for the Liturgy

Music for the Sacred Liturgy

67. "Sacred music is to be considered the more holy the more closely connected it is with the liturgical action, whether making prayer more pleasing, promoting unity of minds, or conferring greater solemnity upon the sacred rites."[65] This holiness involves *ritual* and *spiritual* dimensions, both of which must be considered within *cultural* context.

68. The *ritual dimension* of sacred music refers to those ways in which it is "connected with the liturgical action" so that it accords with the structure of the Liturgy and expresses the shape of the rite. The musical setting must allow the rite to unfold with the proper participation of the assembly and its ministers, without overshadowing the words and actions of the Liturgy.

69. The *spiritual dimension* of sacred music refers to its inner qualities that enable it to add greater depth to prayer, unity to the assembly, or dignity to the ritual. Sacred music is holy when it mediates the holiness of God and forms the Holy People of God more fully into communion with him and with each other in Christ.

---

65   SC, no. 112.

70. The *cultural context* refers to the setting in which the ritual and spiritual dimensions come into play. Factors such as the age, spiritual heritage, and cultural and ethnic background of a given liturgical assembly must be considered. The choice of individual compositions for congregational participation will often depend on those ways in which a particular group finds it best to join their hearts and minds to the liturgical action.

71. With gratitude to the Creator for giving humanity such a rich diversity of musical styles, the Church seeks to employ only that which, in a given style, meets the ritual-spiritual demands of the Liturgy. In discerning the sacred quality of liturgical music, liturgical musicians will find guidance in music from the Church's treasury of sacred music, which is of inestimable value and which past generations have found suitable for worship.[66] They also should strive to promote a fruitful dialogue between the Church and the modern world.[67]

Gregorian Chant

72. "The Church recognizes Gregorian chant as being specially suited to the Roman Liturgy. Therefore, other things being equal, it should be given pride of place in liturgical services."[68] Gregorian chant is uniquely the Church's own music. Chant is a living connection with our forebears in the faith, the traditional music of the Roman rite, a sign of communion with the universal Church, a bond of unity across cultures, a means for diverse communities to participate together in song, and a summons to contemplative participation in the Liturgy.

---

66 See SC, no. 112.

67 "New art forms adapted to our times and in keeping with the characteristics of different nations and regions should be acknowledged by the Church. They may also be brought into the sanctuary whenever they raise the mind up to God with suitable forms of expression and in conformity with liturgical requirements" (GS, no. 62).

68 SC, no. 116.

73. The "pride of place" given to Gregorian chant by the Second Vatican Council is modified by the important phrase "other things being equal."[69] These "other things" are the important liturgical and pastoral concerns facing every bishop, pastor, and liturgical musician. In considering the use of the treasures of chant, pastors and liturgical musicians should take care that the congregation is able to participate in the Liturgy with song. They should be sensitive to the cultural and spiritual milieu of their communities, in order to build up the Church in unity and peace.

74. The Second Vatican Council directed that the faithful be able to sing parts of the Ordinary of the Mass together in Latin.[70] In many worshiping communities in the United States, fulfilling this directive will mean introducing Latin chant to worshipers who perhaps have not sung it before. While prudence, pastoral sensitivity, and reasonable time for progress are encouraged to achieve this end, every effort in this regard is laudable and highly encouraged.

75. Each worshiping community in the United States, including all age groups and all ethnic groups, should, at a minimum, learn *Kyrie XVI*, *Sanctus XVIII*, and *Agnus Dei XVIII*, all of which are typically included in congregational worship aids. More difficult chants, such as *Gloria VIII* and settings of the *Credo* and *Pater Noster*, might be learned after the easier chants have been mastered.[71]

76. "The assembly of the faithful should participate in singing the Proper of the Mass as much as possible, especially through simple responses and other suitable settings."[72] When the congregation does not sing an antiphon or hymn, proper chants from the *Graduale Romanum* might be sung by a choir that is able to render these challenging pieces well. As an easier alternative, chants of the *Graduale Simplex* are recommended.

---

69   MS, no. 50a, further specifies that chant has pride of place "in sung liturgical services celebrated in Latin."
70   "Steps should be taken enabling the faithful to say or to sing together in Latin those parts of the Ordinary of the Mass belonging to them" (SC, no. 54).
71   See GIRM, no. 41. Further resources for congregational Latin chant are *Iubilate Deo* (Vatican City: Libreria Editrice Vaticana, 1986) and *Liber Cantualis* (Sable-sur-Sarthe, France: Abbaye Saint-Pierre de Solesmes, 1983).
72   MS, no. 33.

Whenever a choir sings in Latin, it is helpful to provide the congregation with a vernacular translation so that they are able to "unite themselves interiorly" to what the choir sings.[73]

77. The Entrance and Communion antiphons are found in their proper place in the *Roman Missal*. Composers seeking to create musical arrangements of the appointed antiphons and psalms may also draw from the *Graduale Romanum*, either in their entirety or in shortened refrains for the congregation or choir.

78. Gregorian chant draws its life from the sacred text it expresses, and recent official chant editions employ revised notation suggesting natural speech rhythm rather than independent melodic principles.[74] Singers are encouraged to adopt a manner of singing sensitive to the Latin text.

79. Missals in various languages provide vernacular chants inspired by Latin chant, or other melodies, for sung responses between ministers and people. For the sake of unity across the Church, musicians should not take it upon themselves to adjust or alter these melodies locally.

80. Whenever strophic chant hymns are published with Latin or vernacular texts, their melodies should be drawn from the *Liber Hymnarius*.

The Composer and Music of Our Day

81. The Church needs artists, and artists need the Church. In every age, the Church has called upon creative artists to give new voice to praise and prayer. Throughout history, God has continued to breathe forth his creative Spirit, making noble the work of musicians' hearts and hands. The forms of expression have been many and varied.

---

73   MS, no. 15.
74   The Praenotanda to the 1983 *Liber Hymnarius* explains the flexible rhythms intended by the revised notation.

82. The Church has safeguarded and celebrated these expressions for centuries. In our own day, she continues to desire to bring forth the new with the old. The Church joyfully urges composers and text writers to draw upon their special genius so that she can continue to augment the treasure house of sacred musical art.[75]

83. The Church never ceases to find new ways to sing her love for God each new day. The Sacred Liturgy itself, in its actions and prayers, best makes known the forms in which compositions will continue to evolve. Composers find their inspiration in Sacred Scripture, and especially in the texts of the Sacred Liturgy, so that their works flow from the Liturgy itself.[76] Moreover, "to be suitable for use in the Liturgy, a sung text must not only be doctrinally correct, but must in itself be an expression of the Catholic faith." Therefore, "liturgical songs must never be permitted to make statements about faith which are untrue."[77] Only within this scriptural, liturgical, and creedal context is the composer who is aware of the Church's long journey through human history and "who is profoundly steeped in the *sensus Ecclesiae*" properly equipped "to perceive and express in melody the truth of the Mystery that is celebrated in the Liturgy."[78] No matter what the genre of music, liturgical beauty emanates

---

75   "Then every scribe who has been instructed in the kingdom of heaven is like the head of a household who brings from his storeroom both the new and the old" (Mt 13:52); see USCCB, *Directory on Music and the Liturgy*, awaiting confirmation from the Holy See.

76   Pope John Paul II voiced the charism and praised the work of creative artists in his 1999 *Letter to Artists* (LTA): "None can sense more deeply than you artists, ingenious creators of beauty that you are, something of the pathos with which God at the dawn of creation looked upon the work of his hands. A glimmer of that feeling has shone so often in your eyes when—like the artists of every age— . . . you have admired the work of your inspiration, sensing in it some echo of the mystery of creation with which God, the sole creator of all things, has wished in some way to associate you" (no. 1, *www.vatican.va/holy_father/john_paul_ii/letters/documents/ hf_jp-ii_let_23041999_artists_en.html*).

77   USCCB, *Directory on Music and the Liturgy* (2006), awaiting confirmation from the Holy See.

78   Pope John Paul II, Chirograph of the Supreme Pontiff John Paul II for the Centenary of the Motu Proprio *Tra le Sollecitudini* (*On Sacred Music*), no. 12, *www.vatican. va/holy_father/john_paul_ii/letters/2003/documents/hf_jp-ii_let_20031203_musica- sacra_en.html*.

directly from that mystery and is passed through the talents of composers to emerge in music of the assembled People of God.

84. In the years immediately following the liturgical reforms of the Second Vatican Council, especially because of the introduction of vernacular language, composers and publishers worked to provide a new repertoire of music for indigenous language(s). In subsequent decades, this effort has matured, and a body of worthy vernacular liturgical music continues to develop, even though much of the early music has fallen into disuse. Today, as they continue to serve the Church at prayer, composers are encouraged to concentrate on craftsmanship and artistic excellence in all musical genres.

85. The Church awaits an ever richer song of her entire gathered people. "The faith of countless believers has been nourished by melodies flowing from the hearts of other believers, either introduced into the Liturgy or used as an aid to dignified worship. In song, faith is experienced as vibrant joy, love, and confident expectation of the saving intervention of God."[79]

B. Instruments

The Human Voice

86. Of all the sounds of which human beings, created in the image and likeness of God, are capable, voice is the most privileged and fundamental. Musical instruments in the Liturgy are best understood as an extension of and support for the primary liturgical instrument, which is the human voice.

---

79   LTA, no. 12.

Musical Instruments

87. Among all other instruments which are suitable for divine worship, the organ is "accorded pride of place"[80] because of its capacity to sustain the singing of a large gathered assembly, due to both its size and its ability to give "resonance to the fullness of human sentiments, from joy to sadness, from praise to lamentation." Likewise, "the manifold possibilities of the organ in some way remind us of the immensity and the magnificence of God."[81]

88. In addition to its ability to lead and sustain congregational singing, the sound of the pipe organ is most suited for solo playing of sacred music in the Liturgy at appropriate moments. Pipe organs also play an important evangelical role in the Church's outreach to the wider community in sacred concerts, music series, and other musical and cultural programs. For all of these reasons, the place of the organ should be taken into account from the outset in the planning process for the building or renovation of churches.

89. However, from the days when the Ark of the Covenant was accompanied in procession by cymbals, harps, lyres, and trumpets, God's people have, in various periods, used a variety of musical instruments to sing his praise.[82] Each of these instruments, born of the culture and the traditions of a particular people, has given voice to a wide variety of forms and styles through which Christ's faithful continue to join their voices to his perfect song of praise upon the Cross.

90. Many other instruments also enrich the celebration of the Liturgy, such as wind, stringed, or percussion instruments "according to long-standing local usage, provided they are truly apt for sacred use or can be rendered apt."[83]

---

80   GIRM, no. 393.

81   Pope Benedict XVI, Greeting of the Holy Father on the Occasion of Blessing of the New Organ at Regensburg's Alte Kapelle, Regensburg, Germany (September 13, 2006), www.vatican.va/holy_father/benedict_xvi/speeches/2006/september/documents/hf_ben-xvi_spe_20060913_alte-kapelle-regensburg_en.html.

82   1 Chr 15:20-21.

83   GIRM, no. 393.

Instrumental Music

91. Although instruments are used in Christian worship primarily to lead and sustain the singing of assembly, choir, psalmist, and cantor, they may also, when appropriate, be played by themselves. Such instrumental music can assist the gathering assembly in preparing for worship in the form of a prelude. It may give voice to the sentiments of the human heart through pieces played during the Liturgy and postludes after the Liturgy. Instrumentalists are to remember that the Liturgy calls for significant periods of silent reflection. Silence need not always be filled.

92. Instrumentalists are encouraged to play pieces from the treasury of sacred music by composers of various eras and cultures. In addition, those with the requisite talent and training are encouraged to improvise, as described in no. 43.

Recorded Music

93. Recorded music lacks the authenticity provided by a living liturgical assembly gathered for the Sacred Liturgy. While recorded music might be used advantageously outside the Liturgy as an aid in the teaching of new music, it should not, as a general norm, be used within the Liturgy.

94. Some exceptions to this principle should be noted. Recorded music may be used to accompany the community's song during a procession outside and, when used carefully, in Masses with children. Occasionally, it might be used as an aid to prayer, for example, during long periods of silence in a communal celebration of reconciliation. However, recorded music should never become a substitute for the community's singing.

C. Location of Musicians and Their Instruments

95. Musicians and musical instruments should be located so as to enable proper interaction with the liturgical action, with the rest of the assembly, and among the various musicians. Ideally, ministers of music are located

so as to enable their own full participation by being able to see and hear the Liturgy. In most cases, it will work best if musicians are in close proximity with each other—for example, by placing the organ console or keyboard close to the choir and to the cantor's stand.

96. When not engaged in the direct exercise of their particular role, music ministers, like all ministers of the Liturgy, remain attentive members of the gathered assembly and should never constitute a distraction.

97. The cantor should generally be located in front of the congregation to lead the singing. When a congregation is able to sing on its own, either in response to the priest or ministers or through instrumental leadership, the cantor does not need to be visible. The Responsorial Psalm is usually proclaimed from the ambo or another location that is visible to the assembly. The psalmist, therefore, should sit in a place where the ambo is easily accessible.

98. The placement of the choir should show the choir members' presence as a part of the worshiping community, yet serving in a unique way. Acoustical considerations will also play a role in determining the best location for the choir.

99. Placement of the organ console and pipes, speakers of amplified instruments, and acoustic instruments such as the piano is determined both by visual considerations, so that there is no distraction from the liturgical action, and by acoustical considerations, so that the sound can support the congregation and so that the instrumentalist is readily able to accompany cantors, psalmists, and choirs.

100. If the space occupied by the choir and instruments is visible to the assembly, it must reflect the sacredness of the music ministry. Any appearance of clutter or disorganization must be avoided. Just as no one would tolerate stacks of books and papers in the sanctuary, the music ministry space should be free from clutter.

D. Acoustics

101. Acoustics refers to the quality of a space for sustaining sound, especially its generation, transmission, and reception. While individual ministers of the Liturgy, ensembles, and even choirs can be sound-enhanced through amplification methods, the only amplification of the singing assembly comes from the room itself. Given the primacy of the assembly's song among all musical elements of the Liturgy, the acoustical properties of the worship space are critical. For this reason, specialists in acoustics should be consulted when building or modifying liturgical space.

102. If each member of the assembly senses his or her voice joined to the entire community in a swell of collective sound, the acoustics are well suited to the purpose of a gathered community engaged in sung prayer. If, on the other hand, each person hears primarily only his or her own voice, the acoustics of the space are fundamentally deficient.

103. Sound-absorbing building materials include carpet, porous ceiling tiles, soft wood, untreated soft stone, cast concrete or cinder block, and padded seating. Avoiding excessive use of such materials makes it easier to achieve the ideal of many voices united in song.[84]

104. The acoustics of a church or chapel should be resonant so that there is no need for excessive amplification of musical sound in order to fill the space and support the assembly's song. When the acoustics of the building naturally support sound, acoustic instruments and choirs generally need no amplification. An acoustically dead space precipitates a high cost of sound reinforcement, even for the organ.

---

84   See USCCB, *Built of Living Stones: Art, Architecture, and Worship* (BLS) (Washington, DC: USCCB, 2000), no. 200.

E. Copyrights and Participation Aids

105. Many published works are protected by national and international copyright laws, which are intended to ensure that composers, text writers, publishers, and their employees receive a fair return for their work. Churches and other institutions have a legal and moral obligation to seek proper permissions and to pay for reprinting of published works when required, even if copies are intended only for the use of the congregation.

106. Many publishers provide licenses and other convenient ways for obtaining permission for reprinting texts and music for the use of a liturgical assembly. Pastors, directors of music ministries, and other pastoral musicians need to be informed about the legal requirements for copying printed and recorded music, and they should act with a sense of justice.

107. The United States Conference of Catholic Bishops has delegated to the Committee on Divine Worship the responsibility of overseeing the publication of liturgical books that describe and guide the reformed rites developed in the years since the Second Vatican Council. In light of this responsibility, *Guidelines for the Publication of Participation Aids* has been developed for publishers of popular participation materials.

108. Hymns, songs, and acclamations written for the liturgical assembly are approved for use in the Liturgy by the bishop of the diocese wherein they are published, in order to ensure that these texts truly express the faith of the Church with theological accuracy and are appropriate to the liturgical context.

109. Composers who set liturgical texts to musical settings must respect the integrity of the approved text. Only with the approval of the USCCB Secretariat of Divine Worship may minor adaptations be made to approved liturgical texts.[85]

---

85   See Bishops' Committee on the Liturgy (BCL), *Policy for Approval of Sung Settings of Liturgical Texts*, in *Thirty-Five Years of the BCL Newsletter* (Washington, DC: USCCB, 2004), 1527-1528.

IV. Preparing Music for Catholic Worship

A. What Parts Do We Sing?

The Principle of Progressive Solemnity

110. Music should be considered a normal and ordinary part of the Church's liturgical life. However, the use of music in the Liturgy is always governed by the principle of progressive solemnity.

111. Progressive solemnity means that "between the solemn, fuller form of liturgical celebration, in which everything that demands singing is in fact sung, and the simplest form, in which singing is not used, there can be various degrees according to the greater or lesser place allotted to singing."[86]

112. Progressive solemnity includes not only the nature and style of the music, but how many and which parts of the rite are to be sung. For example, greater feasts such as Easter Sunday or Pentecost might suggest a chanted Gospel, but a recited Gospel might be more appropriate for Ordinary Time. Musical selections and the use of additional instruments reflect the season of the liturgical year or feast that is being celebrated.

113. Solemnities and feasts invite more solemnity. Certain musical selections are more capable of expressing this solemnity, adding an extraordinary richness to these special celebrations. Such solemnity, however,

---

86   MS, no. 7. See *General Instruction of the Liturgy of the Hours* (GILH) (Washington, DC: USCCB, 2002), nos. 271-273.

should never be allowed to devolve to an empty display of ceremony.[87] The most solemn musical expressions retain their primary responsibility of engaging human hearts in the mystery of Christ that is being celebrated on a particular occasion by the Church.

114. At other times, the liturgical season calls for a certain musical restraint. In Advent, for example, musical instruments should be used with moderation and should not anticipate the full joy of the Nativity of the Lord. In Lent, musical instruments should be used only to support the singing of the gathered assembly.[88]

The Parts to Be Sung

115. Singing by the gathered assembly and ministers is important at all celebrations. Not every part that can be sung should necessarily be sung at every celebration; rather "preference should be given to those [parts] that are of greater importance."[89]

a. *Dialogues and Acclamations*

Among the parts to be sung, preference should be given "especially to those to be sung by the priest or the deacon or the lector, with the people responding, or by the priest and people together."[90] This includes dialogues such as *God, come to my assistance. Lord make haste to help me* in the Office, or *The Lord be with you. And also with you* in the Mass. The dialogues of the Liturgy are fundamental because they "are not simply outward signs of communal celebration but foster and bring about communion between priest and people."[91] By their nature, they are short and uncomplicated and easily invite active

---

87   "It should be borne in mind that the true solemnity of liturgical worship depends less on a more ornate form of singing and a more magnificent ceremonial than on its worthy and religious celebration, which takes into account the integrity of the liturgical celebration itself, and the performance of each of its parts according to their own particular nature" (MS, no. 11).

88   See GIRM, no. 313. Exceptions are *Laetare* Sunday, solemnities, and feasts, when a more abundant use of musical instruments is usually appropriate.

89   GIRM, no. 40.

90   GIRM, no. 40; MS, nos. 7 and 16.

91   GIRM, no. 34.

participation by the entire assembly. Every effort should therefore be made to introduce or strengthen as a normative practice the singing of the dialogues between the priest, deacon, or lector and the people. Even the priest with very limited singing ability is capable of chanting *The Lord be with you* on a single pitch.

The acclamations of the Eucharistic Liturgy and other rites arise from the whole gathered assembly as assents to God's Word and action. The Eucharistic acclamations include the Gospel Acclamation, the *Sanctus,* the Memorial Acclamation, and the Great Amen. They are appropriately sung at any Mass, including daily Mass and any Mass with a smaller congregation. Ideally, the people should know the acclamations by heart and should be able to sing them readily, even without accompaniment.

b.   *Antiphons and Psalms*
The psalms are poems of praise that are meant, whenever possible, to be sung.[92] The Psalter is the basic songbook of the Liturgy. Tertullian witnesses to this when he says that in the assemblies of the Christians, "the Scriptures are read, the psalms are sung, sermons are preached."[93] Psalms have a prominent place in every Office of the Liturgy of the Hours.[94]

The Responsorial Psalm in the Liturgy of the Word of the Mass and of other rites "holds great liturgical and pastoral importance, because it fosters meditation on the word of God."[95] The Entrance and Communion chants with their psalm verses serve to accompany the two most important processions of the Mass: the entrance procession, by which the Mass begins, and the Communion procession, by which the faithful approach the altar to receive Holy Communion. Participation in song on the part of the assembly is commended during both of these important processions, as the People of God gather

---

92   See GIRM, no. 102.
93   MSD, no. 10; Tertullian, *De anima,* ch. 9; PL II, 701; and Apol. 39; PL I, 540.
94   "In the liturgy of the hours the Church in large measure prays through the magnificent songs that the Old Testament authors composed under the inspiration of the Holy Spirit. The origin of these verses gives them great power to raise the mind to God, to inspire devotion, to evoke gratitude in times of favor, and to bring consolation and courage in times of trial" (GILH, no. 100).
95   GIRM, no. 61.

at the beginning of Mass and as the faithful approach the holy altar to receive the Body and Blood of the Lord.

c. *Refrains and Repeated Responses*
The Liturgy also has texts of a litanic character that may be sung as appropriate. These include the *Kyrie* and *Agnus Dei* of the Mass, the response to the Prayer of the Faithful at Mass or the intercessions at Morning Prayer and Evening Prayer, and the Litany of the Saints in various rites.

d. *Hymns*
A hymn is sung at each Office of the Liturgy of the Hours, which is the original place for strophic hymnody in the Liturgy. At Mass, in addition to the *Gloria* and a small number of strophic hymns in the *Roman Missal* and *Graduale Romanum*, congregational hymns of a particular nation or group that have been judged appropriate by the competent authorities mentioned in the GIRM, nos. 48, 74, and 87, may be admitted to the Sacred Liturgy. Church legislation today permits as an option the use of vernacular hymns at the Entrance, Preparation of the Gifts, Communion, and Recessional. Because these popular hymns are fulfilling a properly liturgical role, it is especially important that they be appropriate to the liturgical action. In accord with an uninterrupted history of nearly five centuries, nothing prevents the use of some congregational hymns coming from other Christian traditions, provided that their texts are in conformity with Catholic teaching and they are appropriate to the Catholic Liturgy.

116. At daily Mass, the above priorities should be followed as much as possible, in this order: dialogues and acclamations (Gospel Acclamation, *Sanctus*, Memorial Acclamation, Amen); litanies (*Kyrie*, *Agnus Dei*); Responsorial Psalm, perhaps in a simple chanted setting; and finally, a hymn or even two on more important days. Even when musical accompaniment is not possible, every attempt should be made to sing the acclamations and dialogues.

117. Proper antiphons from the liturgical books are to be esteemed and used especially because they are the very voice of God speaking to us in the Scriptures. Here, "the Father who is in heaven comes lovingly to meet his children, and talks with them. And such is the force and power

of the Word of God that it can serve the Church as her support and vigor, and the children of the Church as strength for their faith, food for the soul, and a pure and lasting fount of spiritual life."[96] The Christian faithful are to be led to an ever deeper appreciation of the psalms as the voice of Christ and the voice of his Church at prayer.[97]

Sacred Silence

118. Music arises out of silence and returns to silence. God is revealed both in the beauty of song and in the power of silence. The Sacred Liturgy has its rhythm of texts, actions, songs, and silence. Silence in the Liturgy allows the community to reflect on what it has heard and experienced, and to open its heart to the mystery celebrated. Ministers and pastoral musicians should take care that the rites unfold with the proper ebb and flow of sound and silence.[98] The importance of silence in the Liturgy cannot be overemphasized.

B. Who Prepares the Music for the Liturgy?

119. Preparation for the celebration of the Sacred Liturgy, and particularly for the selection of what is to be sung at the Liturgy, is ultimately the responsibility of the pastor and of the priest who will celebrate the Mass.[99] At the same time, "in planning the celebration of Mass, [the priest] should have in mind the common spiritual good of the people of God, rather than his own inclinations."[100]

---

96   Second Vatican Council, *Dei Verbum* (*Dogmatic Constitution on Divine Revelation*) (DV) (1965), no. 21.

97   "The praying of the psalms . . . must be grasped with new warmth by the people of God. This will be achieved more readily if a deeper understanding of the psalms, in the meaning in which they are used in the liturgy, is more diligently promoted among the clergy and communicated to all the faithful by means of appropriate catechesis" (Paul VI, Apostolic Constitution *Laudis Canticum* [1970], no. 8).

98   See nos. 91, 94, 151, 176, 199, 209, 215, 243, and 249.

99   See GIRM, no. 111.

100   GIRM, no. 352.

120. In order that there "be harmony and diligence in the effective preparation of each liturgical celebration in accord with the *Missal* and other liturgical books,"[101] the pastor may designate that the director of music or a Liturgy or music committee meet regularly to make the preparations necessary for a good use of the available liturgical and musical options.

121. When a Liturgy or music committee is chosen to prepare music for the Liturgy, it should include persons with the knowledge and artistic skills needed in celebration: men and women trained in Catholic theology, Liturgy, and liturgical music and familiar with current resources in these areas. It is always good to include as consultants some members of the worshiping assembly so that their perspective is represented.

C. Care in the Choice of Music for the Liturgy

122. Music for the Liturgy must be carefully chosen and prepared. Such preparation should be characterized by "harmony and diligence . . . under the direction of the rector [or pastor] of the Church and after the consultation with the faithful about things that directly pertain to them."[102] Effective preparation of liturgical song that fosters the maximum participation of the gathered assembly is a cooperative venture that respects the essential role of a variety of persons with mutual competencies.

123. Each particular liturgical celebration is composed of many variable verbal and non-verbal elements: proper prayers, scriptural readings, the liturgical season, the time of day, processional movement, sacred objects and actions, the socio-economic context in which the particular community is set, or even particular events impacting the life of the Christian faithful. Every effort should be made to lend such disparate elements a

---

101   GIRM, no. 111.
102   GIRM, no. 111.

certain unity by the skillful and sensitive selection and preparation of texts, music, homily, movement, vesture, color, environment, and sacred objects and actions. This kind of ritual art requires that those who prepare the Liturgy approach it with artistic sensitivity and pastoral perspective.

124. Music does what words alone cannot do. It is capable of expressing a dimension of meaning and feeling that words alone cannot convey. While this dimension of an individual musical composition is often difficult to describe, its affective power should be carefully considered along with its textual component.

125. The role of music is to serve the needs of the Liturgy and not to dominate it, seek to entertain, or draw attention to itself or the musicians. However, there are instances when the praise and adoration of God leads to music taking on a far greater dimension. At other times, simplicity is the most appropriate response. The primary role of music in the Liturgy is to help the members of the gathered assembly to join themselves with the action of Christ and to give voice to the gift of faith.

D. Judging the Qualities of Music for the Liturgy

The Three Judgments: One Evaluation

126. In judging the appropriateness of music for the Liturgy, one will examine its liturgical, pastoral, and musical qualities. Ultimately, however, these three judgments are but aspects of one evaluation, which answers the question: "Is this particular piece of music appropriate for this use in this particular Liturgy?" All three judgments must be considered together, and no individual judgment can be applied in isolation from the other two. This evaluation requires cooperation, consultation, collaboration, and mutual respect among those who are skilled in any of the three judgments, be they pastors, musicians, liturgists, or planners.

The Liturgical Judgment   *Does it fit?*

127. The question asked by this judgment may be stated as follows: Is this composition capable of meeting the structural and textual requirements set forth by the liturgical books for this particular rite?

128. Structural considerations depend on the demands of the rite itself to guide the choice of parts to be sung, taking into account the principle of progressive solemnity (see nos. 110ff. in this document). A certain balance among the various elements of the Liturgy should be sought, so that less important elements do not overshadow more important ones. Textual elements include the ability of a musical setting to support the liturgical text and to convey meaning faithful to the teaching of the Church.

129. A brief introduction to the aspects of music and the various liturgical rites is provided below in nos. 137ff. Pastoral musicians should develop a working familiarity with the requirements of each rite through a study of the liturgical books themselves.

The Pastoral Judgment   *can it be done?*

130. The pastoral judgment takes into consideration the actual community gathered to celebrate in a particular place at a particular time. Does a musical composition promote the sanctification of the members of the liturgical assembly by drawing them closer to the holy mysteries being celebrated? Does it strengthen their formation in faith by opening their hearts to the mystery being celebrated on this occasion or in this season? Is it capable of expressing the faith that God has planted in their hearts and summoned them to celebrate?

131. In the dioceses of the United States of America today, liturgical assemblies are composed of people of many different nations. Such peoples often "have their own musical tradition, and this plays a great part in their religious and social life. For this reason their music should be

held in proper esteem and a suitable place is to be given to it, not only in forming their religious sense but also in adapting worship to their native genius. . . ."[103]

132. Other factors—such as the age, culture, language, and education of a given liturgical assembly—must also be considered. Particular musical forms and the choice of individual compositions for congregational participation will often depend on those ways in which a particular group finds it easiest to join their hearts and minds to the liturgical action. Similarly, the musical experience of a given liturgical assembly is to be carefully considered, lest forms of musical expression that are alien to their way of worshiping be introduced precipitously. On the other hand, one should never underestimate the ability of persons of all ages, cultures, languages, and levels of education to learn something new and to understand things that are properly and thoroughly introduced.

133. The pastoral question, finally, is always the same: Will this composition draw this particular people closer to the mystery of Christ, which is at the heart of this liturgical celebration?

The Musical Judgment *Is it good?*

134. The musical judgment asks whether this composition has the necessary aesthetic qualities that can bear the weight of the mysteries celebrated in the Liturgy. It asks the question: Is this composition technically, aesthetically, and expressively worthy?

135. This judgment requires musical competence. Only artistically sound music will be effective and endure over time. To admit to the Liturgy the cheap, the trite, or the musical cliché often found in secular popular songs is to cheapen the Liturgy, to expose it to ridicule, and to invite failure.

---

103   SC, no. 119.

136. Sufficiency of artistic expression, however, is not the same as musical style, for "the Church has not adopted any particular style of art as her own. She has admitted styles from every period, in keeping with the natural characteristics and conditions of peoples and the needs of the various rites."[104] Thus, in recent times, the Church has consistently recognized and freely welcomed the use of various styles of music as an aid to liturgical worship.

---

104   SC, no. 123.

V. The Musical Structure of Catholic Worship

A. Music and the Structure of the Mass

137. Those responsible for preparing music for the celebration of the Eucharist in accord with the three preceding judgments must have a clear understanding of the structure of the Liturgy. They must be aware of what is of primary importance. They should know the nature of each of the parts of the Mass and the relationship of each part to the overall rhythm of the liturgical action.

138. The Mass is made up of the Liturgy of the Word and the Liturgy of the Eucharist. Although each has its own distinctive character, these two parts are so closely connected as to form one act of worship. "The Church is nourished spiritually at the twofold table of God's word and of the Eucharist:[105] from the one it grows in wisdom and from the other in holiness."[106] In addition, the Mass has introductory and concluding rites.

The Introductory Rites

139. The first part of the Mass consists of rites that "have the character of a beginning, introduction, and preparation."[107] They include an Entrance

---

105   See SC, no. 51; Second Vatican Council, *Presbyterorum Ordinis* (*Decree on the Ministry and Life of Priests*) (1965), no. 18; DV, no. 21; AG, no. 6; GIRM, no. 8.
106   LFM, no. 10.
107   GIRM, no. 46.

chant or song, the reverencing of the altar, a greeting of the people, an Act of Penitence and the *Kyrie* (or the Sprinkling Rite), *Gloria*, and Collect.

140. These rites are designed "to ensure that the faithful who come together as one establish communion and dispose themselves to listen properly to God's word and to celebrate the Eucharist worthily."[108] So that the people might come together as one, it is appropriate that they always sing at least one piece as a congregation in the introductory rites—Entrance song or chant, *Kyrie*, or *Gloria*—apart from the sung dialogues of the Liturgy.

141. On certain occasions, such as Palm Sunday, or when the other sacraments or rites are celebrated at Mass, some of these rites are omitted or celebrated in a particular manner that requires variations in the choice of music. Those responsible for the musical preparation of the Liturgy must be aware of these variations in practice.

The Entrance Chant or Song
142. After the entire liturgical assembly has been gathered, an Entrance chant or song is sung as the procession with the priest, deacon, and ministers enters the church. "The purpose of this chant is to open the celebration, foster the unity of those who have been gathered, introduce their thoughts to the mystery of the liturgical season or festivity, and accompany the procession of the priest and ministers."[109]

143. Care must be taken in the treatment of the texts of psalms, hymns, and songs in the Liturgy. Verses and stanzas should not be omitted arbitrarily in ways that risk distorting their content. While not all musical pieces require that all verses or stanzas be sung, verses should be omitted only if the text to be sung forms a coherent whole.

---

108   GIRM, no. 46.
109   GIRM, no. 47.

144. The text and music for the Entrance song may be drawn from a number of sources.

a. The singing of an antiphon and psalm during the entrance procession has been a long-standing tradition in the Roman Liturgy. Antiphons and psalms may be drawn from the official liturgical books—the *Graduale Romanum*, or the *Graduale Simplex*—or from other collections of antiphons and psalms.

b. Other hymns and songs may also be sung at the Entrance, providing that they are in keeping with the purpose of the Entrance chant or song. The texts of antiphons, psalms, hymns, and songs for the Liturgy must have been approved either by the United States Conference of Catholic Bishops or by the local diocesan bishop.[110]

The Act of Penitence
145. After the greeting, the Act of Penitence follows as the entire assembly prays a formula of general confession.[111] When the third form of the Act of Penitence is sung (e.g., "You were sent to heal the contrite: Lord, have mercy . . . ") variable invocations of Christ's mercy may be chosen.[112]

The Kyrie Eleison
146. The ancient invocation *Kyrie* is a "chant by which the faithful acclaim the Lord and implore his mercy."[113] If the *Kyrie* is not included

---

110   "The singing at this time is done either alternately by the choir and the people or in a similar way by the cantor and the people, or entirely by the people, or by the choir alone. In the dioceses of the United States of America there are four options for the Entrance Chant (song): (1) the antiphon from the *Roman Missal* or the Psalm from the *Roman Gradual* as set to music there or in another musical setting; (2) the seasonal antiphon and Psalm of the *Simple Gradual*; (3) a song from another collection of psalms and antiphons, approved by the Conference of Bishops or the diocesan Bishop, including psalms arranged in responsorial or metrical forms; (4) a suitable liturgical song similarly approved by the Conference of Bishops or the diocesan Bishop" (GIRM, no. 48).

111   See GIRM, no. 51.

112   See GIRM, no. 52.

113   GIRM, no. 52.

in the Act of Penitence, it is sung or said immediately afterwards. It is usually sung in dialogue by the entire liturgical assembly with the choir or cantor.

The Blessing and Sprinkling of Water
147. "On Sundays, especially in the Season of Easter, in place of the customary Act of Penitence, from time to time the blessing and sprinkling of water to recall Baptism may take place."[114] The blessing of the water may be sung. The song accompanying the sprinkling with blessed water should have an explicitly baptismal character.

The Gloria
148. "The *Gloria* is a very ancient and venerable hymn in which the Church, gathered together in the Holy Spirit, glorifies and entreats God the Father and the Lamb. The text of this hymn may not be replaced by any other text. . . . It is sung or said on Sundays outside the Seasons of Advent and Lent, on solemnities and feasts, and at special celebrations of a more solemn character."[115]

149. The priest, or the cantor or choir, intones the *Gloria*. It is sung by all, by the people alternately with the choir or cantor, or by the choir alone. If not sung, it is recited either by all together or by two parts of the congregation in alternation. While through-composed settings of the *Gloria* give clearest expression to the text, the addition of refrains is permitted, provided the refrains encourage congregational participation.[116]

150. The *Gloria* may not be moved to a different part of the Mass than the one assigned by the *Roman Missal*. It may not, for example, be used in place of the Entrance chant or song, or during the sprinkling with blessed water.

---

114   GIRM, no. 51; see *The Roman Missal*, Appendix II.
115   GIRM, no. 53.
116   BCL, *Policy for the Approval of Sung Settings of Liturgical Texts*.

The Collect

151. The priest then invites all to pray and, after a brief silence, sings or says the Collect.[117] Even when the Collect is not sung, the conclusion to the prayer may be sung, along with the response by the people.

The Liturgy of the Word

152. The Liturgy of the Word consists of readings and responses from Sacred Scripture.[118] In receiving the Word of God with their hearts and minds, and in responding to it in song, "the people make God's Word their own."[119]

The Readings from Sacred Scripture

153. While the readings are ordinarily read in a clear, audible, and intelligent way,[120] they may also be sung. "This singing, however, must serve to bring out the sense of the words, not obscure them."[121]

154. Even if the readings are not sung, the concluding acclamation *The Word of the Lord* may be sung, even by someone other than the reader; all respond with the acclamation *Thanks be to God*. "In this way the assembled congregation pays reverence to the word of God it has listened to in faith and gratitude."[122]

The Responsorial Psalm

155. The Responsorial Psalm follows the first reading. Because it is an integral part of the Liturgy of the Word, and is in effect a reading from Scripture, it has great liturgical and pastoral significance.[123] Corresponding to the reading that it follows, the Responsorial Psalm is intended to

---

117   See GIRM, no. 54.

118   GIRM, no. 55.

119   GIRM, no. 55.

120   See LFM, no. 14.

121   "On occasions when the readings are in Latin, the manner of singing given in the *Ordo cantus Missae* is to be maintained" (LFM, no. 14).

122   LFM, no. 18.

123   LFM, nos. 19-22; see GIRM, no. 61.

foster meditation on the Word of God. Its musical setting should aid in this, being careful to not overshadow the other readings.[124]

156. "As a rule the Responsorial Psalm should be sung."[125] Preferably, the Psalm is sung responsorially: "the psalmist, or cantor of the psalm, sings the psalm verses and the whole congregation joins in by singing the response."[126] If this is not possible, the Psalm is sung completely without an intervening response by the community.

157. The proper or seasonal Responsorial Psalm from the *Lectionary for Mass*, with the congregation singing the response, is to be preferred to the gradual from the *Graduale Romanum*.[127] When the Latin gradual is sung *in directum* (straight through) by choir alone, the congregation should be given a vernacular translation.

158. Because the Psalm is properly a form of sung prayer, "every means available in each individual culture is to be employed"[128] in fostering the singing of the Psalm at Mass, including the extraordinary options provided by the *Lectionary for Mass*. In addition to the proper or seasonal Psalm in the *Lectionary*, the Responsorial Psalm may also be taken from the *Graduale Romanum* or the *Graduale Simplex*, or it may be an antiphon and psalm from another collection of the psalms and antiphons, including psalms arranged in paraphrase or in metrical form, providing that they have been approved by the United States Conference of Catholic Bishops or the diocesan bishop.

159. Songs or hymns that do not at least paraphrase a psalm may never be used in place of the Responsorial Psalm.[129]

---

124 See LFM, no. 19.
125 LFM, no. 20.
126 LFM, no. 20.
127 "The Responsorial Psalm should correspond to each reading and should, as a rule, be taken from the Lectionary" (GIRM, no. 61; see LFM, nos. 20, 89).
128 LFM, no. 21.
129 See GIRM, no. 61.

160. If it is not possible for the Psalm to be sung, the response alone may be sung, while the lector reads the intervening verses of the Psalm "in a manner conducive to meditation on the word of God."[130]

The Gospel Acclamation

161. In the Gospel Acclamation, the assembled faithful welcome "the Lord who is about to speak to them."[131] The cantor may intone the Acclamation, which is repeated by the whole assembly. After the cantor or choir sings the verse, the entire assembly again sings the Acclamation. If there is a Gospel procession, the Acclamation may be repeated as often as necessary to accompany the Gospel procession. The verses are as a rule taken from the *Lectionary for Mass*.

162. The Gregorian settings of the Gospel Acclamation are most appropriate for use in those communities which are able to sing the response communally.[132]

163. During most of the church year, the *Alleluia* with the proper verse serves as the Gospel Acclamation. During the season of Lent, alternate acclamations with their proper verse are used, as found in the *Lectionary for Mass* (or, when there is only one reading before the Gospel, the Psalm alone may be used). The Gospel Acclamation may be omitted when it is not sung.

164. When there is only one reading before the Gospel, the Gospel Acclamation may be omitted; if it is a season in which the *Alleluia* is said, the *Alleluia* may be used as the response of the Psalm, or the Psalm with its proper response may be used followed by the *Alleluia* with its verse. The Gospel Acclamation may be omitted when it is not sung.[133]

The Sequence

165. The Sequence is a liturgical hymn that is sung before the Gospel Acclamation on certain days. On Easter Sunday (*Victimae paschali laudes*)

---

130   LFM, no. 22; see LFM, no. 21.
131   LFM, no. 23.
132   GIRM, no. 62, "[The Gospel Acclamation] is sung by all while standing."
133   GIRM, no. 63.

and Pentecost Day (*Veni Sancte Spiritus*), the Sequence is required.[134] On the Solemnity of the Most Holy Body and Blood of the Lord (*Lauda Sion Salvatorem*) and Our Lady of Sorrows (*Stabat Mater*), the Sequence is optional.

166. The Sequence may be sung by all together, or in alternation between the congregation and choir and cantor, or by the choir or cantor alone. The text from the *Lectionary for Mass* may be used, or a metrical paraphrase may be sung, provided that it is found in an approved collection of liturgical songs.

The Gospel

167. "Of all the rites connected with the Liturgy of the Word, the reverence due to the Gospel reading must receive special attention."[135]

168. While the Gospel is ordinarily proclaimed in a clear, audible, and intelligent way,[136] it may also be sung.[137] "This singing, however, must serve to bring out the sense of the words, not obscure them."[138]

169. "Even if the Gospel itself is not sung, it is appropriate for the greeting *The Lord be with you*, and *A reading from the holy Gospel according to . . .* , and at the end *The Gospel of the Lord* to be sung, in order that the congregation may also sing its acclamations. This is a way both of bringing out the importance of the Gospel reading and of stirring up the faith of those who hear it."[139]

The Creed

170. The Creed is said by the entire assembly. Because it is an expression of faith by "the whole gathered people,"[140] the participation of all present should be carefully safeguarded, whether it is said or sung. "If it is sung, it

---

134   GIRM, no. 64.

135   LFM, no. 17.

136   LFM, no. 14.

137   On occasions when the Gospel is in Latin, the manner of singing given in the *Ordo cantus Missae* is to be maintained. (See LFM, no. 14.)

138   LFM, no. 14.

139   LFM, no. 17.

140   GIRM, no. 67.

is begun by the Priest or, if this is appropriate, by a cantor or by the choir. It is sung, however, either by all together or by the people alternating with the choir."[141] The use of a congregational refrain may be helpful in this regard.

The Prayer of the Faithful
171. The Prayer of the Faithful consists of intercessions by which "the people respond in a certain way to the word of God which they have welcomed in faith and, exercising the office of their baptismal priesthood, offer prayers to God for the salvation of all."[142] Because it has the structure of a litany, and provided that it can be understood when sung, it is appropriate to sing the Prayer of the Faithful, or just the invitation and response, or even the response only.

The Liturgy of the Eucharist

172. The Liturgy of the Eucharist is made up of three main parts: the Preparation of the Gifts, the Eucharistic Prayer, and the Communion Rite.[143]

The Preparation of the Gifts: Offertory Procession
173. After the altar has been prepared, gifts of bread and wine are brought to the priest or deacon by members of the liturgical assembly. This procession is accompanied by an Offertory chant or song,[144] "which continues at least until the gifts have been placed on the altar."[145] The norms on the manner of singing are the same as for the Entrance chant (see nos. 142ff. in this document).

174. Even when there is no procession with the gifts, singing may still accompany the rites at the Offertory.[146] Instrumental music is also appropriate.

---

141   GIRM, no. 68.
142   GIRM, no. 69. See LFM, nos. 31 and 53.
143   See GIRM, no. 72.
144   See GIRM, nos. 37b, 111.
145   GIRM, no. 74.
146   See GIRM, no. 74.

175. The priest then prays the Prayer over the Offerings. Even when the prayer is not sung, the conclusion to the prayer may be sung, along with the response by the people.

The Eucharistic Prayer
176. The Eucharistic Prayer is the center and summit of the entire celebration. Joining the people with himself, the priest prays the Eucharistic Prayer in the name of the entire assembly "to God the Father through Jesus Christ in the Holy Spirit."[147] Through the Eucharistic Prayer "the entire congregation of the faithful should join itself with Christ in confessing the great deeds of God and in the offering of sacrifice. The Eucharistic Prayer demands that all listen to it with reverence and in silence,"[148] giving voice to their interior participation by joining in the Eucharistic acclamations.

177. The Eucharistic Prayer is a single liturgical act, consisting of several parts: an introductory dialogue, the thanksgiving or preface, the *Sanctus*, the calling down of the Holy Spirit (*epiclesis*), the institution narrative, the Memorial Acclamation, the anamnesis, the offering, the intercessions, and the doxology with its Amen.[149]

178. In order to make clear the ritual unity of the Eucharistic Prayer, it is recommended that there be a stylistic unity to the musical elements of the prayer, especially the *Sanctus*, the Memorial Acclamation, and the Great Amen. As much as possible, elements such as the preface dialogue and preface should be chanted at a pitch that best relates them to the key and modality of the other sung elements of the Eucharistic Prayer.

179. The Eucharistic Prayer begins with a dialogue between the priest and the people that expresses their communion with one another in offering the Eucharistic sacrifice. The faithful "give thanks to God and offer the spotless Victim not only through the hands of the Priest but also together

---

147   See GIRM, no. 78.
148   GIRM, no. 78.
149   See GIRM, no. 79.

with him."[150] Because the preface dialogue is among the most important dialogues of the Mass, it is very appropriate that it be sung, especially on Sundays and other solemn occasions.[151]

180. The people take part in the Eucharistic Prayer by listening attentively to the words sung or spoken by the priest and joining their hearts and minds to the actions of the prayer. Their voices should be joined together in the acclamations of the Eucharistic Prayer, including the *Sanctus*, the great cosmic acclamation of praise; the Memorial Acclamation, by which the faithful participate in keeping the memory of Christ's Paschal Mystery; and the Amen that follows the concluding doxology, by which they give assent to the entire prayer. These acclamations should be sung, especially on Sundays and solemnities.[152]

181. Because the Eucharistic Prayer is the central action of the entire celebration, priests should, if possible, sing at least those parts for which musical notation is provided in the *Roman Missal*, at least on Sundays and on more solemn occasions. These parts include the opening dialogue and the Preface, the invitation to the Memorial Acclamation, and the concluding doxology. It is not permitted to recite the Eucharistic Prayer inaudibly while the *Sanctus* is sung.

182. It is likewise appropriate for priests to sing the entire Eucharistic Prayer, especially on solemn occasions. The chant setting provided in the *Roman Missal* or another composition approved by the United States Conference of Catholic Bishops may be used. "While the Priest proclaims the Eucharistic Prayer 'there should be no other prayers or singing, and the organ or other musical instruments should be silent,' except for the people's acclamations."[153]

---

150   GIRM, no. 95.

151   See GIRM, no. 40.

152   See GIRM, no. 40.

153   Congregation for Divine Worship and the Discipline of the Sacraments, *Redemptionis Sacramentum* (*Instruction on the Eucharist*), no. 53 (Washington, DC: USCCB, 2004).

183. "It is a praiseworthy practice for the parts that are to be said by all the concelebrants together and for which musical notation is provided in the Missal to be sung."[154]

The Communion Rite

184. The high point of the Communion Rite is the reception of Holy Communion. This is preceded by rites that prepare the faithful to receive the Lord's Body and Blood as spiritual food.[155]

185. The Lord's Prayer and the Sign of Peace are followed by the Breaking of the Bread, "which gave the entire Eucharistic Action its name in apostolic times" and which "signifies that the many faithful are made one body (1 Cor 10:17) by receiving Communion from the one Bread of Life which is Christ, who died and rose for the salvation of the world."[156] This Fraction Rite, accompanied by the *Agnus Dei* chant, is followed by the *Ecce Agnus Dei* and the reception of Holy Communion. The Communion Rite concludes with the Prayer after Communion.

The Lord's Prayer

186. The rites of preparation for the reception of Holy Communion begin with the Lord's Prayer. When the Lord's Prayer is sung, the doxology should also be sung by all. If possible, the invitation and embolism should also be sung by the priest.

The Sign of Peace

187. The brief period of time needed for the exchange of the Sign of Peace must not be protracted by the singing of a song.

The Fraction Rite and the *Agnus Dei*

188. The supplicatory chant *Agnus Dei* accompanies the Fraction Rite. It is, "as a rule, sung by the choir or cantor with the congregation responding; or it is, at least, recited aloud. This invocation accompanies the fraction and, for this reason, may be repeated as many times as necessary

---

154   GIRM, no. 218.
155   See GIRM, no. 80.
156   GIRM, no. 83.

until the rite has reached its conclusion, the last time ending with the words *dona nobis pacem* (*grant us peace*)."[157] When the *Agnus Dei* is sung repeatedly as a litany, Christological invocations with other texts may be used. In this case, the first and final invocations are always *Agnus Dei* (Lamb of God).

The Communion Chant or Song

189. "While the priest is receiving the Sacrament, the Communion chant [or song] is begun. Its purpose is to express the communicants' union in spirit by means of the unity of their voices, to show joy of heart, and to highlight more clearly the 'communitarian' nature of the procession to receive Communion."[158] The singing begins immediately and continues "for as long as the Sacrament is being administered to the faithful."[159] The Communion chant or song may be sung by the people with choir or cantor, or by the choir alone. Because the Communion chant expresses the unity of those processing and receiving the Holy Sacrament, communal singing is commendable. The singing of the people should be preeminent.

190. There are several options for the Communion song or chant,[160] including the proper antiphon from the *Graduale Romanum*, a seasonal antiphon from the *Graduale Simplex*,[161] an antiphon and psalm from a collection approved for liturgical use, or another appropriate liturgical song.[162]

---

157 GIRM, no. 83.

158 GIRM, no. 86.

159 GIRM, no. 86.

160 "In the dioceses of the United States of America there are four options for the Communion chant (song): (1) the antiphon from the Roman Missal or the Psalm from the *Roman Gradual*, as set to music there or in another musical setting; (2) the seasonal antiphon and Psalm of the *Simple Gradual*; (3) a song from another collection of psalms and antiphons, approved by the United States Conference of Catholic Bishops or the diocesan Bishop, including psalms arranged in responsorial or metrical forms; (4) a suitable liturgical song chosen in accordance with no. 86. This is sung either by the choir alone or by the choir or cantor with the people" (GIRM, no. 87).

161 Antiphons from the *Graduale Romanum* or *Graduale Simplex* might be sung in Latin or vernacular.

162 See GIRM, no. 87.

191. In selecting a Communion song suitable for the Eucharistic banquet in which God's blessings are bestowed so abundantly, one should look for texts that have themes of joy, wonder, unity, gratitude, and praise. Following ancient Roman liturgical tradition, the Communion song might reflect themes of the Gospel reading of the day. It is also appropriate to select a Communion processional song that reflects the liturgical action, i.e., eating and drinking the Body and Blood of Christ.

192. As a processional piece, the Communion chant or song presents particular challenges. The faithful are encouraged to grasp ever more deeply the essentially communitarian nature of the Communion procession. In order to foster participation of the faithful with "unity of voices," it is recommended that psalms sung in the responsorial style, or songs with easily memorized refrains, be used. The refrains will generally need to be limited in number and repeated often, especially at the outset, so that they become familiar to the faithful.

193. When the Communion procession is lengthy, more than one piece of music might be desirable. In this case, there may be a combination of pieces for congregation and pieces for choir alone. Choirs with the requisite ability may sing the proper Communion chant from the *Graduale Romanum*, either in Gregorian chant or in a polyphonic setting, or other suitable choral pieces. Instrumental music may also be used to foster a spirit of unity and joy. If there is a hymn or song after Communion, the Communion music should be ended "in a timely manner."[163] A period of silent reflection for the entire congregation after the reception of Communion is also appropriate.

194. During the various seasons of the year, the psalm or song during Communion should be chosen with the spirit of that season in mind. On most Sundays and other days, it would be appropriate to sing one of the psalms that have long been associated with participation in the Eucharistic banquet, such as Psalms 23, 34, and 147. There is also a substantial repertory of liturgical songs that give expression to the joy and wonder of sharing in the Lord's Supper.

---

163   GIRM, no. 86.

204. During the Rite of Election, ordinarily celebrated on the First Sunday of Lent, an appropriate psalm or song may be sung during the enrollment of names, as catechumens sign the Book of the Elect.

205. The Scrutinies are ordinarily celebrated during the Sunday Masses of the Third, Fourth, and Fifth Sundays of Lent. The texts for these Masses are always drawn from Year A of the *Lectionary*. At the conclusion of the exorcism rite, all may join in singing an appropriate psalm or song.

206. During the Easter Vigil, the three Sacraments of Initiation—Baptism, Confirmation, and the Eucharist—are ordinarily celebrated. The assembly should join in singing responses and acclamations during the Litany of the Saints, the acclamations for and at the conclusion of the blessing prayer over the baptismal water, and the acclamations following each Baptism. There may be a song between the celebration of Baptism and Confirmation, especially if the neophytes need to change into dry clothing or if there is a procession from the font to the sanctuary. A song may also be sung during Confirmation as the neophytes are anointed with chrism, especially if a large number of persons are being confirmed.

The Baptism of Children

207. It is important to recall the unique circumstances that often accompany the Baptism of children, along with the importance of singing envisioned by these rites. For this and certain other sacraments, cantors and other ministers will often need to develop the skill of leading unaccompanied singing.

208. In the beginning of the rite, "the people may sing a psalm or hymn suitable for the occasion" as the celebrating priest or deacon, accompanied by the ministers, "goes to the entrance of the church or the part of the church where the parents and godparents are waiting with those who are to be baptized."[169] After questioning the parents and godparents and signing the forehead of the children, the celebrant invites all those

---

169   *Rite of Baptism for Children* (RBC), in *The Rites*, no. 35 (New York: Pueblo Publishing, 1976); see RBC, nos. 74, 107.

present to take part in the Liturgy of the Word. Then "there is a procession to the place where this will be celebrated, during which a song is sung, e.g., Psalm 85:7, 8, 9ab."[170]

209. After the homily or, if there is no homily, after the litany invoking the intercession of the saints, "it is desirable to have a period of silence while all pray at the invitation of the celebrant. If convenient, a suitable song follows."[171] After the prayer of exorcism and the anointing before Baptism, if the baptistery is located outside the church or is not in view of the congregation, all should process to the baptistery while an appropriate song is sung, for example, Psalm 23.[172] The Rite of Baptism also allows for the possibility that the Profession of Faith may be followed by a suitable song "by which the community expresses its faith with a single voice."[173] Furthermore, after each Baptism, the rite indicates that "it is appropriate for the people to sing a short acclamation."[174]

210. Following the celebration of the sacrament, those who have been baptized are clothed in a white garment and given a candle, which has been lit from the Easter candle. If there is an exceptionally large number of children, the people may sing a song until each child has a candle.[175] Once this has been done, everyone processes to the altar while singing a "baptismal song."[176] Following the Lord's Prayer, the blessing, and the dismissal, "all may sing a hymn which suitably expresses thanksgiving and Easter joy, or they may sing the song of the Blessed Virgin Mary, the Magnificat."[177] Chapter VII in the *Rite of Baptism for Children* offers numerous acclamations and hymns that may be used during the Liturgy.[178]

---

170   RBC, no. 42; see no. 80.
171   RBC, no. 46; see no. 83.
172   See RBC, no. 52.
173   RBC, no. 59; see no. 96.
174   RBC, no. 60; see nos. 97, 125.
175   See RBC, no. 127.
176   RBC, no. 67; see no. 102.
177   RBC, no. 71; see nos. 106, 131.
178   See RBC, nos. 225-245.

The Baptism of Children During Sunday Mass

211. Baptism may be celebrated during Mass on Sunday, "so that the entire community may be present and the relationship between baptism and Eucharist may be clearly seen; but this should not be done too often."[179]

212. When the Rite of Baptism of Children is celebrated at Mass, music for the rite should be included. Among the parts that may be sung are an opening antiphon or processional song during the Introductory Rites; the intercessions and Litany of the Saints following the homily; and an acclamation following the Profession of Faith. Furthermore, after each child is baptized, the people may sing a short acclamation.

The Sacrament of Confirmation

213. Given this sacrament's importance, the Rite of Confirmation urges that "attention should be paid to the festive and solemn character of the liturgical service and its significance for the local church."[180] Since, as a rule, the celebration of Confirmation takes place within Mass, music during the Liturgy of Confirmation should follow the guidelines already mentioned above in nos. 137-199.[181]

214. Additionally, the Rite of Confirmation suggests that the Profession of Faith may be followed by a suitable song in which "the community may express its faith."[182] Likewise, one or more songs may be sung while the bishop anoints those to be confirmed, such as Veni Creator Spiritus.[183]

215. If the Sacrament of Confirmation is being celebrated outside Mass, in addition to the moments mentioned above, "all may sing a psalm or appropriate song" while the bishop goes to the sanctuary with the other ministers.[184] During the Liturgy of the Word, two or three readings are

179   RBC, no. 9.
180   Rite of Confirmation (RC) (Washington, DC: USCCB, 2006), no. 4.
181   See RC, no. 13.
182   RC, no. 23; see no. 40.
183   See RC, nos. 29, 46.
184   RC, no. 34.

used following the traditional order (a reading from the Old Testament or the Acts of the Apostles [during the Easter season], an epistle from the New Testament, and a Gospel). "After the first and second reading there should be a psalm or song, or a period of silence may be observed."[185]

The Rite of Marriage

216. The lifelong bond established by the marriage covenant between a man and a woman derives its force from creation. Jesus Christ has raised this natural covenant to a higher dignity as a sacrament of the new and eternal covenant.[186] Above all else, the "grace of Christian marriage is a fruit of Christ's cross, the source of all Christian life."[187]

217. "According to the Latin tradition, the spouses as ministers of Christ's grace mutually confer upon each other the Sacrament of Matrimony by expressing their consent before the Church."[188] Therefore, while the celebration of marriage concerns the spouses and their families, it is not only a private matter. Since their consent is given in the presence of the Church, the celebration of marriage is governed by the appropriate liturgical norms. The Church desires that a person's wedding day be filled with joy and grace. When preparing the Liturgy, pastors should address any concerns with the couple with due pastoral sensitivity and sound judgment.

218. The preparation of the Liturgy must concern not only those involved but also the norms of the ritual itself.[189] The marriage Liturgy presents particular challenges and opportunities to planners. Both musicians and pastors should make every effort to assist couples to understand and

---

185 RC, no. 37.
186 See *Code of Canon Law: Latin-English Edition: New English Translation* (*Codex Iuris Canonici*) (CIC) (Washington, DC: Canon Law Society of America, 1998), can. 1055, §1; GS, no. 48, §1.
187 CCC, no. 1615.
188 CCC, no. 1623.
189 See *Rite of Marriage* (RM), nos. 28-32, from the *Ordo Celebrandi Matrimonium*, editio typica altera (Typis Polyglottis Vaticanis, 1990). While this second edition of the *Rite of Marriage* has not yet been published in an English edition, the rubrics of the Latin edition are current liturgical law.

share in the planning of their marriage Liturgy. Since oftentimes the only music familiar to the couple is not necessarily suitable to the sacrament, the pastoral musician will make an effort to demonstrate a wide range of music appropriate for the Liturgy.

219. It is helpful for a diocese or a parish to have a definite but flexible policy that provides clear guidance and also allows for pastoral sensitivity regarding wedding music. This policy should be communicated early to couples as a normal part of their preparation in order to avoid last-minute crises and misunderstandings.

220. Particular decisions about choice and placement of wedding music should be based on the three judgments proposed above (see nos. 126ff.): the liturgical judgment, the pastoral judgment, and the musical judgment. As indicated previously, all three of these judgments must be taken into account, since they are aspects of a single judgment. Additionally, music should reflect the truth that all the sacraments celebrate the Paschal Mystery of Christ.[190] Secular music, even though it may emphasize the love of the spouses for one another, is not appropriate for the Sacred Liturgy. Songs that are chosen for the Liturgy should be appropriate for the celebration and express the faith of the Church.[191]

221. If vocal soloists are to be employed in the celebration of the sacrament, they should be instructed on the nature of the Liturgy and trained in the unique aspects of singing in a liturgical context. Either the soloist should be trained to carry out the ministry of psalmist and cantor, or else another singer should be secured for this liturgically important role. In all cases, soloists should be aware that their talents are offered at the service of the Liturgy. Vocalists may sing alone during the Preparation of the Gifts or after Communion, provided the music and their manner of singing does not call attention to themselves but rather assists in the contemplation of the sacred mysteries being celebrated. Soloists should not usurp parts of the Mass designated for congregational participation.

---

190   See SC, no. 61; CCC, no. 1621.
191   See RM, no. 30; SC, nos. 118, 121.

222. If the Rite of Marriage is celebrated within Mass, the norms for music within Mass as described in nos. 137-199 of this document apply. The entrance procession—consisting of the ministers, attendants, witnesses, bride, and groom—is accompanied by a suitable song or instrumental music. If instrumental music is played, the assembly may join in a song once all have taken their places. The Liturgy of the Word proceeds as usual with a Responsorial Psalm, which may be sung. Following the homily, the sacrament is celebrated with the exchange of consent and the Church's reception of consent. After the blessing and exchanging of rings, a song or hymn of praise may be sung.[192] Depending on the local custom and the culture of the families, after the exchange of rings, the veiling of the bride and groom and other customary actions may be added, during which an appropriate psalm or song may be sung.

223. When, for pastoral reasons, the sacrament is celebrated outside of Mass, the Liturgy should begin with an entrance song or instrumental piece.[193] If instrumental music is played, the assembly may join in a song once all have taken their places. The Liturgy of the Word takes place in the usual manner, with the possibility of singing a Responsorial Psalm.[194] Following the homily, the sacrament is celebrated with the exchange of consent and the Church's reception of consent. After the blessing and exchanging of rings, a song or hymn of praise may be sung.[195] When the sacrament is celebrated outside of Mass but Communion is distributed, a chant or song may accompany the distribution of the sacrament, as well as the period of thanksgiving after Communion is distributed.[196]

224. Since the celebration of marriage is a communal celebration, participation aids should be provided to the congregation so that they might follow the ritual with understanding. This, in turn, allows them to have full and active participation in the celebration. Participation aids should include especially those elements of the Liturgy unique to the marriage rite, as well as translations of any songs not sung in the vernacular. Such

---

192   See RM, no. 64.
193   See RM, nos. 78-79.
194   See RM, no. 83.
195   See RM, no. 94.
196   See RM, nos. 131, 133.

participation aids should also include proper copyright notices for permission to use copyrighted music in the program.

The Rites of Ordination

225. For the ordination of bishops, priests, or deacons, an "entrance antiphon with its psalm or another suitable liturgical song is sung" at the beginning of the Liturgy.[197] Once the bishop receives the promises of those elected to orders, the Litany of Supplication is sung as the elect prostrate themselves.[198]

226. As the newly ordained are clothed in the vestments of their order, an antiphon is sung with its proper psalm as indicated in the rite.[199] Otherwise, "another appropriate liturgical song of the same kind with suitable antiphon may be sung."[200] This is especially appropriate if the psalm indicated in the rite has already been used during the Liturgy of the Word.[201] The *Rites of Ordination* suggests that a second antiphon and a second psalm be sung during the kiss of peace.[202] Here, too, another appropriate liturgical song may be substituted.[203] Finally, "a liturgical song of thanksgiving may be sung after the distribution of Communion."[204]

The Sacrament of Anointing of the Sick

227. When the Sacrament of Anointing of the Sick takes place within a large congregation, "the full participation of those present must be fostered by every means, especially through the use of appropriate songs, so that the celebration manifest[s] the Easter joy which is proper to this Sacrament."[205]

---

197 *Rites of Ordination of a Bishop, of Priests, and of Deacons* (ORD) (Washington, DC: USCCB, 2003), no. 118; see ORD, no. 195.

198 See ORD, nos. 127, 203.

199 See ORD, nos. 134, 209.

200 See ORD, nos. 134, 209.

201 See ORD, nos. 134, 209.

202 See ORD, nos. 137, 212.

203 See ORD, nos. 137, 212.

204 ORD, no. 142; see no. 217.

205 *Pastoral Care of the Sick* (PCS), no. 108, in *The Rites*.

228. "When the condition of the sick person permits, and especially when communion is to be received, the Sacrament of Anointing may be celebrated within Mass."[206] Music for the Mass should be selected in accordance with the norms set forth above and with sensitivity to the nature and locale of the celebration. Musical settings for the litany may be developed. Additionally, if large numbers of sick persons are present, instrumental music may be played as the priest anoints each of them.

The Sacrament of Penance

229. The Rite for Reconciliation of Several Penitents with Individual Confession and Absolution normally requires an entrance song or song of gathering; a Responsorial Psalm and a Gospel Acclamation during the Liturgy of the Word; an optional hymn after the homily; and a hymn of praise for God's mercy following the absolution. The litany within the General Confession of Sins (alternating between the deacon or cantor and the assembly) or another appropriate song may also be sung, as well as the Lord's Prayer. Singing or soft instrumental music may be used during the time of individual confessions, especially when a large number of people is present for the celebration.

C. Music and the Liturgy of the Hours

230. The public celebration of the Liturgy of the Hours, especially Morning and Evening Prayer, sanctifies time and participates in the prayer of Christ and his Church. Such celebrations should foster "the active participation of all according to their individual circumstances through acclamations, dialogues, alternating psalmody and other things of this kind, and takes into account various forms of expression. . . . In this way the wish of the Apostle is fulfilled: 'Let the word of Christ dwell in

---

206   PCS, no. 131.

you richly, as in all wisdom you teach and admonish one another, sing-ing psalms, hymns, and spiritual songs with gratitude in your hearts to God.'"[207]

231. As much as possible, communal celebration of the Liturgy of the Hours with singing is to be preferred to private recitation.[208] Those bound to the Office are reminded that private recitation is commended only when communal celebration is not possible. The hours are not to be anticipated but are to be celebrated at their proper times.[209]

232. The psalms and canticles should be sung whenever possible. The *General Instruction of the Liturgy of the Hours* lists several ways in which the psalms may be sung: responsorially, antiphonally, or straight through (*in directum*). Music may be of the formula type (e.g., psalm tones) or through-composed for each psalm or canticle.

Responsorial

233. The responsorial form of psalm singing appears to have been the original style for congregational use and still remains an excellent method for engaging the congregation in the singing of psalms. In this model, the psalmist or choir sings the verses of the psalm, and the assembly responds with a brief antiphon (refrain). For pastoral or musical reasons, the *General Instruction* permits the substitution of other approved texts for these refrains.

Antiphonal

234. In the antiphonal style, the praying assembly is divided into two groups. The text of the psalm is shared between them; generally the same musical configuration (e.g., a psalm tone) is used by both. A refrain is ordinarily sung before and after the psalm by the whole body. This method of singing has its roots in the choir and monastic traditions. Today, where

---

207   Col 3:16; see Eph 5:19-20; GILH, no. 33.
208   See SC, nos. 99, 100, 101.
209   See SC, no. 94.

it is used by the congregation, care must be taken that the people can be at ease with this form of sung prayer.

Through-Composed

235. In a through-composed setting (*in directum*), the musical material is ordinarily not repeated, unless the psalm calls for it. The music may be for soloist, soloist and choir, or choir alone (e.g., an anthem). Only rarely will this form be found in settings designed for congregational use. The purpose of the *in directum* setting should be to complement the literary structure of the psalm and to capture its emotions.

Metrical Psalms

236. A metrical psalm is a psalm text that has been transformed into a strophic hymn with a recurring metrical structure, such that its stanzas can be sung to a hymn melody. Metrical psalmody has been a part of Protestant and Catholic practice ever since the sixteenth century. Due to its four-hundred-year tradition, a large and important repertoire of metrical psalms in English is available today. Poets and composers continue to add to this resource of psalm settings. In order to foster the sung rendition of psalms, metrical psalmody may be used in the Liturgy of the Hours, provided that the metrical text is faithful to the sacred text of the original psalm.

Formula Tones

237. Formula tones (newly written psalm tones, Anglican chants, faux-bourdons) are readily available and well suited for vernacular texts. Care should be taken when setting vernacular texts so that the verbal accent pattern is not distorted by the musical cadence. Gregorian chant tones are suited to the Latin language, which does not, for the most part, have accents on the final syllable of a line. For this reason, Gregorian tones should generally not be used for those vernacular languages that have final accents, or else the Gregorian cadences should be adapted to fit the accentuation of the vernacular language.

238. Where formula tones are employed for the hours of the Divine Office, especially with a parish congregation, variety should be sought in

Order of Christian Funerals

The Importance of Music in the Order of Christian Funerals

244. The Church's funeral rites offer thanksgiving to God for the gift of life that has been returned to him. Following ancient custom, the funeral rites consist of three stages or stations that are joined by two processions. In Christian Rome, "Christians accompanied the body on its last journey. From the home of the deceased the Christian community proceeded to the church singing psalms. When the service in the church concluded, the body was carried in solemn procession to the grave or tomb."[214] Throughout the liturgies, the ancient Christians sang psalms and antiphons praising God's mercy and entrusting the deceased to the angels and the saints.[215]

245. The psalms are given pride of place in the funeral rites because "they powerfully express the suffering and pain, the hope and trust of people of every age and culture. Above all the psalms sing of faith in God, of revelation and redemption."[216] Effective catechesis will allow communities to understand the significance of the psalms used in the funeral rites.

246. Sacred music has an integral role in the funeral rites, since it can console and uplift mourners while, at the same time, uniting the assembly in faith and love.[217] Funeral music should express the Paschal Mystery and the Christian's share in it.[218] Since music can evoke strong feelings, it should be chosen with care. It should console the participants and "help to create in them a spirit of hope in Christ's victory over death and in the Christian's share in that victory."[219] Secular music, even though it may reflect on the background, character, interests, or personal preferences of the deceased or mourners, is not appropriate for the Sacred Liturgy.

---

214   *Order of Christian Funerals* (OCF) (New York: Catholic Book Publishing Co., 1989), no. 42.
215   See OCF, no. 42.
216   OCF, no. 25.
217   See OCF, no. 30.
218   See OCF, no. 30.
219   OCF, no. 31.

247. Music should be provided for the vigil and funeral Mass. Whenever possible, music should accompany the funeral processions and the rite of committal.[220] For the processions, preference should be given to "settings of psalms and songs that are responsorial or litanic in style and that allow the people to respond to the verses with an invariable refrain."[221]

248. Music should never be used to memorialize the deceased, but rather to give praise to the Lord, whose Paschal Sacrifice has freed us from the bonds of death.

The Vigil for the Deceased

249. If the Vigil for the Deceased is celebrated with the body's reception at the church, a special rite is used.[222] The minister, with the assisting ministers, meets the coffin at the door of the church; and the coffin is sprinkled with holy water and the pall is placed, the entrance procession begins and proceeds to the place the coffin will occupy. "During the procession a psalm, song, or responsory is sung."[223] The Vigil for the Deceased then proceeds as usual and may conclude with silence or a song.[224]

250. After the minister greets those present, the Vigil for the Deceased begins with a song.[225] Following the opening prayer, the Liturgy of the Word begins. For the Responsorial Psalm, "Psalm 27 is sung or said or another psalm or song."[226] Silence or a song may conclude the vigil.[227]

251. The rite for the transfer of the body to the church or to the place of committal includes an invitation to prayer, a brief reading of Scripture, a litany, the Lord's Prayer, and a concluding prayer. Following the concluding prayer, the minister invites those present to join the procession to the church or the place of committal. "During the procession, psalms and

---

220   See OCF, nos. 32, 41.
221   OCF, no. 41.
222   See OCF, nos. 82-97.
223   OCF, no. 85.
224   See OCF, no. 97.
225   See OCF, no. 70.
226   OCF, no. 75.
227   See OCF, no. 81.

other suitable songs may be sung. If this is not possible, a psalm is sung or recited either before or after the procession." The rite specifically suggests Psalm 122 with its provided antiphon.[228]

The Funeral Liturgy

252. If the body has not yet been received at the church, the priest, with the assisting ministers, meets the coffin at the door of the church; and after the coffin is sprinkled with holy water and the pall is placed, the entrance procession begins moving to the place the coffin will occupy. "During the procession a psalm, song, or responsory is sung" while the priest and ministers take their place in the sanctuary.[229]

253. Unless it is to be celebrated at the place of committal, the final commendation follows the Prayer After Communion. After the invitation to prayer, the song of farewell is sung.[230]

254. "The song of farewell, which should affirm hope and trust in the paschal mystery, is the climax of the rite of final commendation. It should be sung to a melody simple enough for all to sing. It may take the form of a responsory or even a hymn."[231] If the song of farewell is sung, it is not recited.

255. Following the prayer of commendation, the deacon or priest invites those present to join the procession to the place of committal. One or more of the psalms provided by the rite may be sung during the procession to the entrance of the church. If convenient, singing may continue during the journey to the place of committal. The psalms particularly appropriate for this procession are Psalms 25, 42, 93, 116, 118, and 119.[232]

---

228   OCF, no. 127.
229   OCF, no. 162.
230   See OCF, no. 174.
231   OCF, no. 147.
232   See OCF, no. 176.

Rite of Committal

256. The rite of committal is the conclusion of the funeral rite and is celebrated at the grave, tomb, mausoleum, or crematorium. It may also be used for burial at sea.[233] The rite begins with an invitation to prayer and is followed by a Scripture verse, a prayer over the place of committal, intercessions, the Lord's Prayer, a concluding prayer, and finally a prayer over the people. A song may conclude the rite.[234]

257. The practice of developing funeral choirs within parish communities should be encouraged. The funeral choir is commonly made up of individuals who tend to be available on weekday mornings and who gather to lend their collective voice in support of the assembly song at the funeral Mass.

E. Devotions

258. "Sacred music is also very effective in fostering the devotion of the faithful in celebrations of the word of God, and in popular devotions. . . . In all popular devotions the psalms will be especially useful, and also works of sacred music drawn from both the old and the more recent heritage of sacred music, popular religious songs, and the playing of the organ, or of other instruments characteristic of a particular people. Moreover, in these same popular devotions, and especially in celebrations of the word of God, it is excellent to include as well some of those musical works which, although they no longer have a place in the liturgy, can nevertheless foster a religious spirit and encourage meditation on the sacred mystery."[235]

---

233   See OCF, nos. 204ff., 316.
234   See OCF, no. 326.
235   MS, no. 46.

VI. Conclusion

259. As the Church in the United States continues its journey of liturgical renewal and spiritual growth, we hope that this document will be a further encouragement in our progress along that course. The words of St. Augustine remind us of our pilgrimage: "You should sing as wayfarers do—sing but continue your journey. Do not grow tired, but sing with joy!"[236]

---

236   St. Augustine, *Sermo* 256, 1.2.3 (PL 38, 1191-1193).

Acknowledgments

Scripture texts used in this work are taken from the *New American Bible*, copyright © 1991, 1986, and 1970 by the Confraternity of Christian Doctrine, Washington, DC 20017, and are used by permission of the copyright owner. All rights reserved.

Excerpts from the *Catechism of the Catholic Church*, second edition, copyright © 2000, Libreria Editrice Vaticana–United States Conference of Catholic Bishops, Washington, DC. Used with permission. All rights reserved.

Excerpts from *Vatican Council II: The Conciliar and Post Conciliar Documents* edited by Austin Flannery, OP, copyright © 1975, Costello Publishing Company, Inc., Northport, NY, are used with permission of the publisher, all rights reserved. No part of these excerpts may be reproduced, stored in a retrieval system, or transmitted in any form or by any means—electronic, mechanical, photocopying, recording, or otherwise—without express written permission of Costello Publishing Company.

Excerpts from the English translation of *Rite of Baptism for Children* © 1969, International Committee on English in the Liturgy, Inc. (ICEL); excerpts from the English translation of *The Roman Missal* © 1973, ICEL; excerpts from the English translation of *The Liturgy of the Hours* © 1974, ICEL; excerpts from the English translation of *Holy Communion and Worship of the Eucharist Outside Mass* © 1974, ICEL; excerpts from the English translation of *Rite of Confirmation*, Second Edition © 1975, ICEL; excerpts from the English translation of the Introduction from *Lectionary for Mass* © 1981, 1997, ICEL; excerpts from the English translation of *Pastoral Care of the Sick: Rites of Anointing and Viaticum* © 1982, ICEL; excerpts from *Order of Christian Funerals* © 1985, ICEL; excerpts from the English translation of *Rite of Christian Initiation of Adults* © 1985, ICEL;excerpts from the English translation of *Rites of Ordination of a Bishop, of Priests, and of Deacons* © 2000, 2002, ICEL; excerpts from the English translation of *General Instruction of the Roman Missal* © 2002, ICEL. All rights reserved.

Excerpts from John Paul II, *Letter to Artists* © 1999 Libreria Editrice Vaticana (LEV), Vatican City; excerpts from Sacred Congregation for Rites, *Musicam Sacram* (*Instruction on Music in the Liturgy*) © 1967 LEV; excerpts from Pius XII, *Musicae Sacrae Disciplina* (*On Sacred Music*) © 1955 LEV; excerpts from Pope Benedict XVI, *Sacramentum Caritatis* (*Sacrament of Charity*) © 2007 LEV; excerpts from Pope John Paul II, Address to Bishops of the Northwest Provinces of the USCCB © 1998 LEV; excerpts from Pope John Paul II, Chirograph of the Supreme Pontiff John Paul II for the Centenary of the Motu Proprio *Tra le Sollecitudini* (*On Sacred Music*) © 2003 LEV; excerpts from Pope Benedict XVI, Greeting of the Holy Father on the Occasion of Blessing of the New Organ at Regensburg's Alte Kapelle © 2006 LEV; excerpts from Congregation for Divine Worship and the Discipline of the Sacraments, *Redemptionis Sacramentum* (*Instruction on the Eucharist*) © 2004 LEV; excerpts from Sacred Congregation for Rites, *Eucharisticum Mysterium* (*Instruction on the Worship of the Eucharistic Mystery*) © 1967 LEV. Used with permission. All rights reserved.

Index

According to Paragraph Numbers